THIRD EDITION

TOP NOTCH

FUNDAMENTALS

ENGLISH FOR TODAY'S WORLD

JOAN SASLOW
ALLEN ASCHER

With *Top Notch Pop* Songs and Karaoke
by Rob Morsberger

Top Notch: English for Today's World   Fundamentals, Third Edition

Pearson Education, 10 Bank Street, White Plains, NY 10606 USA

Staff credits: The people who made up the *Top Notch* team are Peter Benson, Kimberly Casey, Jennifer Castro, Tracey Munz Cataldo, Rosa Chapinal, Aerin Csigay, Dave Dickey, Gina DiLillo, Nancy Flaggman, Irene Frankel, Shelley Gazes, Christopher Leonowicz, Julie Molnar, Laurie Neaman, Sherri Pemberton, Pamela Pia, Rebecca Pitke, Jennifer Raspiller, Charlene Straub, and Kenneth Volcjak.

Cover photo: Sprint/Corbis
Text composition: TSI Graphics

Library of Congress Cataloging-in-Publication Data

Saslow, Joan M.
  Top Notch : English for today's world. Fundamentals / Joan Saslow, Allen Ascher ; With Top Notch Pop Songs
  and Karaoke by Rob Morsberger. — Third Edition.
      pages cm
  Includes biographical references.
  ISBN 978-0-13-354275-2 — ISBN 978-0-13-339348-4 — ISBN 978-0-13-354277-6 — ISBN 978-0-13-354278-3   1. English language —
  Textbooks for foreign speakers. 2. English language—Problems, exercises, etc. 3. English language — Sound recordings for foreign
  speakers. I. Ascher, Allen. II. Morsberger, Robert Eustis, 1929- III. Title. IV. Title: English for today's world.
  PE1128.S2757 2015
  428.2'4 — dc23

                        2013044020

Printed in the United States of America
ISBN-10: 0-13-392791-1
ISBN-13: 978-0-13-392791-7
1 2 3 4 5 6 7 8 9 10—V003—19 18 17 16 15

ISBN-10: 0-13-354275-0 (with MyEnglishLab)
ISBN-13: 978-0-13-354275-2 (with MyEnglishLab)
2 3 4 5 6 7 8 9 10—V003—19 18 17 16 15

pearsonelt.com/topnotch3e

In Memoriam

Rob Morsberger (1959–2013)

The authors wish to acknowledge their memory of and gratitude to **Rob Morsberger**, the gifted composer and songwriter of the *Top Notch Pop* Songs and Karaoke that have provided learners both language practice and pleasure.

hoto credits: Original photography by Sharon Hoogstraten and David Mager. Page 4 (1) Rido Franz/iStock/Thinkstock/Getty Images, (2) WaveBreakMedia/Shutterstock, 3) Iceteastock/Fotolia, (4) Fancy Collection/SuperStock, (5) Val Thoermer/Fotolia, (6) Nisakorn Neera/Fotolia, (7) Andrey Kiselev/Fotolia, (8) Tony Freeman/PhotoEdit, Inc., (9) Darrin enry/Fotolia, (10) Andres Rodriguez/Fotolia; p. 5 (actor) Everett Collection/Alamy, (singer) Infusl-v07/INFphoto.com/Newscom, (musician) Benjamin Harte/ArenaPal/The Image Works, athlete) News Free/CON/LatinContent/Getty Images; p. 6 (1) Michael Jung/Fotolia, (2) Hero Images/AGE Fotostock, (3) Fotek/Fotolia, (4) Laviejasirena/Fotolia, (5) Minerva Studio/Fotolia, 5) Lev/Fotolia, (7) Byrdyak/Fotolia, (8) Pixel974/Fotolia; p. 8 (top) Donatas1205/Fotolia; p. 10 (actor)Peter Brooker/Rex Features/Press select/Alamy, (singer) Jason Merrit/Getty Images, athlete) Top Photo/Courtesy Everett Col/USA Rights Only/ Everett Collection/Alamy, (writer) Jeremy Sutton-Hibbert/Alamy; p. 13 (top) Felix Mizioznikov/Fotolia; p. 14 (top) Monkey usiness Images/Shutterstock, (1) Nicholas Piccillo/Fotolia, (2) Minerva Studio/Fotolia, (3) Hfng/Fotolia, (4) Monkey Business/Fotolia, (5) Tyler Olson/Fotolia, (6) Monart Design/Fotolia; . 18 (chef) Jean Ayissi/AFP/Getty Images/Newscom, (musician) Tina Lau/Splash News/Newscom, (athlete) Daniel Munoz/Reuters/Newscom, (writer) Tara Walton/Toronto Star/Getty nages, (singer) AFP/Getty Images, (actor) Splash News/Corbis, (bottom left) Felix Mizioznikov/Fotolia, (bottom middle) Mykeyruna/Fotolia; p. 19 (bottom)Stocklite/Shutterstock; p. 20) Chuck Savage/Corbis, (2) CandyBox Images/Fotolia, (3) JGI/Tom Grill/Blend Images/Alamy, (4) Paolo Bona/AGE Fotostock, (5) Steve Hamblin/Alamy, (6) India Images/Dinodia Photos/ lamy; p. 22 (1) Mimagephotos/Fotolia, (2) Michael Jung/Fotolia, (3) Stephen Coburn/Fotolia, (4) Connel/Shutterstock, (5) John. A. Rizzo/Photodisc/Thinkstock/Getty Images, (middle left) hipfactory/Shutterstock, (walk) Mimagephotos/Fotolia, (don't-drive) Michael Jung/Fotolia; p. 23 (middle left) JGI/Tom Grill/Blend Images/Alamy, (middle) Steve Hamblin/Alamy, (middle ght) India Images/Dinodia Photos/Alamy, (bottom left) CandyBox Images/Fotolia, (bottom middle) Paolo Bona/AGE Fotostock, (bottom right) Chuck Savage/Corbis; p. 24 (1) Algre/ otolia, (2) Tarasov_vl/Fotolia, (3) Tuatong/Fotolia, (4) Marcin-Linfernum/Shutterstock, (5) Tsach/Fotolia; p. 26 (1) Iofoto/Fotolia, (2) Eurobanks/Fotolia, (3) BananaStock/Thinkstock/Getty nages, (4) Phovoir/YAY Media AS/Alamy; p. 28 (background) Dmitrydesigner/Fotolia (top 2) Monkey Business/Fotolia, (top 3) Monkey Business/Fotolia, (top 5) Monkey Business/Fotolia, op 6) Monkey Business/Fotolia, (top 8) Monkey Business/Fotolia, (top 9) Monkey Business/Fotolia, (top 11, 12) Monkey Business/Fotolia, (top 13, 14) Monkey Business/Fotolia, (top 15, 6) Monkey Business/Fotolia, (bottom 1a) Elena Stepanova/Fotolia, (bottom 1b) Stuart Monk/Fotolia, (bottom 2a) Volker Witt/Fotolia, (bottom 2b) Elena Stepanova/Fotolia, (bottom 3a) uliya Chsherbakova/istock/Thinkstock/Getty Images, (bottom 3b) Stuart Monk/Fotolia, (bottom 4a) Goodluz/Fotolia, (bottom 4b) Monkey Business/Fotolia, (bottom 5a) Igor Mojzes/ otolia, (bottom 5b) Nadezda Postolit/Fotolia, (bottom 6a) Kirill Kedrinski/Fotolia, (bottom 6b) Tanya Ustenko/Shutterstock; p. 29 WaveBreakMedia/Shutterstock; p. 30 (top 1, 2) Gary alter/Corbis, (top 3, 4) Sergey Khamidulin/Fotolia, (top 5) Infusny-142/Jennifer Graylock/INFphoto.com/Newscom, (top 6) Everett Collection/Newscom, (top 8) Ana Blazic Pavlovic/ otolia, (bottom 1) Yupiramos Group/Fotolia, (bottom 2) Kenishirotie/Fotolia, (bottom 3) Monkey Business Images/Shutterstock; p. 31 (4) Antony Nagelmann/The Image Bank/Getty nages, (5) Mimagephotos/Fotolia, (6) Edyta Pawlowska/Fotolia, (bottom right) Bikeriderlondon/Shutterstock; p. 32 (top right) Igor Mojzes/Fotolia; p. 33 (top) Citizen Stock/Blend Images/ lamy, (bottom) Diego Cervo/Shutterstock; p. 34 (left) Redcarpetpress/Alamy, (middle) BFA/SIPA/Newscom, (right) TPG Top Photo Group/Newscom, (right) ChinaFotoPress/Getty Images; . 35 (background) Dmitrydesigner/Fotolia, (right) Monkey Business/Fotolia, (left) Micromonkey/Fotolia; p. 38 (1) ColorBlind Images/Glow Images, (2) Juergen Henkelmann Photography/ lamy, (3) Mike Powell/Allsport Concepts/Getty Images, (4) Emmanuel Lattes/Alamy, (5a) Danr13/Fotolia, (5b) Boscorelli/Fotolia, (6) Olly/Fotolia; p. 39 (dance) Chuck Savage/Corbis, asketball) Julián Rovagnati/Fotolia, (space shuttle) Vadim Sadovski/Shutterstock, (dinner) Sugar0607/Fotolia, (concert) Galina Barskaya/Fotolia; p. 41 (top) Christopher Bailey/Alamy, ottom) Jan Tyler/iStock/Thinkstock/Getty Images; p. 42 (party) Monkey Business/Fotolia, (movie) United Artists/Album/Newscom, (dance) WaveBreakMediaMicro/Fotolia, (meeting) ıse/Fotolia, (game) Galina Barskaya/Fotolia; p. 43 (dinner) Kathy Burns-Millyard/Fotolia, (basketball) .Shock/Fotolia, (concert) Andrey Armyagov/Fotolia; p. 44 (1) Heinteh/Fotolia,) Ruslan Kudrin/Fotolia, (3) Andersphoto/Fotolia, (4) Alexandra Karamyshev/Fotolia, (5) Ahturner/Shutterstock, (6) Elnur/Fotolia, (7) Andrey_Arkusha/Fotolia, (8) (Left) Ken Hurst/Fotolia, ight) Alliance/Fotolia, (9,10) Phil Date/Thinkstock/Getty Images; p. 46 (1-10) Kenishirotie/Fotolia; p. 47 (top) Nicholas Eveleigh/Getty Images, (Top Left) Pavel L Photo and Video/ hutterstock, (Top Right) Pavel L Photo and Video/Shutterstock, (pant) Voltan/Fotolia, (tie) Photoblink/Fotolia, (male suit) Kayros Studio/Fotolia, (female suit) Dmitry Vereshchagin/Fotolia, lue skirt) Nikita Buida/Fotolia, (orange jacket) Ivan Gulei/Fotolia, (black shoe) Siwi1/Fotolia; p. 48 (1) Uluc Ceylani/Shutterstock, (2) Cloki/Shutterstock, (3) Vichly4thai/Fotolia,) Vichly4thai/Fotolia , (7) Elnur/Fotolia, (8) Elnur/Fotolia, (9) Yo/Fotolia, (10) Serkucher/Fotolia; p. 49 BananaStock/Thinkstock/Getty Images; p. 50 (Top Left) Theartofphoto/Fotolia, op Center) Robert Lehmann/Fotolia, (Top Right) Daniel Escalise/Fotolia, Andrey Bandurenko/Fotolia; p. 55 Minerva Studio/Fotolia, p. 57 DreamPictures/Getty Images, p. 58 (Roomba) leksiy Maksymenko Photography/Alamy, (Scooba) S_E/Fotolia, (center left) Xinhua/Photoshot/Newscom, (center) DC5 WENN Photos/Newscom, (center right) Presselect/Alamy; p. 59 op background) Eugenesergeev/ Fotolia, (bottom background) Narongsak Yaisumlee/Shutterstock; p. 61 (1) WavebreakMediaMicro/Fotolia, (2) Snaptitude/Fotolia, (3) Monkey Business/ otolia, (4) Daniel Ernst/Thinkstock/Getty Images, (5) East/Shutterstock, (6) Lightwavemedia/Fotolia; p. 63 (dance) Chuck Savage/Corbis, (bottom right) Chad Baker/Jason Reed/Ryan cVay/Photodisc/Getty Images; p. 65 (1) Javier Larrea/AGE Fotostock, (2) Dmitry Pistrov /Fotolia, (3) Frank Boston/Fotolia, (4) Ed Brennan/Fotolia, (5) Janine Wiedel Photolibrary/Alamy,) Robert Harding World Imagery/Alamy, (7) Shutterbas/Fotolia, (8) Spotmatikphoto/Fotolia; p. 67 (top left) Bartok007/Fotolia, (top right) MasterLu/Fotolia; p. 69 (red chair) Amadorgs/ otolia, (mirror) Anna Biancoloto/Shutterstock, (brown lamp) Zerbor/Fotolia, (mat) Africa Studio/Fotolia, (household) Mrgarry/Fotolia; p. 70 (bg) Artur Bogacki /Fotolia, (left) Imtmphoto/ otolia, (middle) Bevangoldswain/Fotolia, (right) Antonio Nunes/Fotolia; p. 75 Tetra Images/AGE Fotostock; p. 77 Maridav/Fotolia; p. 81 (green bean salad) Marco Mayer/Fotolia, (Fruit lad) Matthias Krapp/Shutterstock, (tomato potato soup) Robert6666/Fotolia, (potato pancake) Kolazig/Fotolia, (stuffed peppers) M.studio/Fotolia; p. 92 (1) Haveseen/Fotolia, (2) Rido/ otolia, (3) Purestock/Getty Images, (4) Michael Jung/Fotolia, (5) Claro Alindogan/iStock/Thinkstock/Getty Images, (6) Bikeriderlondon/Shutterstock; p. 94 (top left) Fotoluminate LLC/ otolia, (middle left) Szefei/iStock/Thinkstock/Getty Images, (bottom left) Nyul/Fotolia, (bottom right) Nejron Photo/Shutterstock; p. 96 (1) Creativa/Fotolia, (2) Sanneberg/Fotolia,) Alinute/Fotolia, (4) Goodluz/Fotolia, (5) Digitalefotografien/Fotolia, (6) Contrastwerkstatt/Fotolia, (9) BigLike Images/Fotolia, (10) Auremar/Fotolia, (12) Zea Lenanet/Fotolia, 3) Eurobanks/Fotolia, (top right) Jose Manuel Gelpi Diaz/Hemera/Thinkstock/Getty Images, (bottom left) Jeanette Dietl/Fotolia, (3a) Siri Stafford/Photodisc/Getty Images, (3c) 2/Mel urtis/Ocean/Corbis, (3d) Peter Atkins/Fotolia; p. 97 (Sangalo) Andrea Comas/Reuters/Newscom, (Bocelli) Allen Berezovsky/WireImage/Getty Images, (Adams) Derek Ross/LFI/Photoshot/ ewscom, (Sandé) Infusny-261/AlbertoReyes/INFphoto.com/Newscom, (Hemsworth) BT1 WENN Photos/Newscom; p. 98 (12, 13, 14) Christian Schwier/Fotolia, (15, 16, 17) Vibe Images/ otolia; p. 100 (1) JupiterImages/Pixland/Thinkstock/Getty Images, (2) Nyul/Fotolia, (3) Mirkoni/Shutterstock, (4 see a doctor) WaveBreakMediaMicro/Fotolia, (4 see a dentist) agonImages/Fotolia; p. 102 (top left) Baverel-Lefranc/Kipa/Corbis, (middle left) ZUMA Press, Inc./Alamy, (top right) Cortesia Notimex/Newscom, (middle right) Jean Catuffe, cificCoastNews/Newscom; p. 105 (top left) Edyta Pawlowska/Fotolia, (top right) Studio-Annika/iStock/Thinkstock/Getty Images; p. 107 (middle right) Cusp/SuperStock, (lunch) or Mojzes/Fotolia, (walk) Michael Jung/Fotolia, (cycling) Purestock/Getty Images, (driving) Bikeriderlondon/Shutterstock; p. 113 (1) John Neubauer/PhotoEdit, Inc., (2) Uwimages/Fotolia,) Michael Jung/Fotolia, (4) Apops/Fotolia, (5) Igor Mojzes/Fotolia, (6) Mitarart/Fotolia, (7) Andres Rodriguez/Fotolia, (8) Michael Jung/Fotolia, (9) Michael Jung/Fotolia, (10) APG/Alamy, ottom right) Stuart Jenner/Shutterstock; p. 115 (top right) Arek_malang/Shutterstock, (driving) Bikeriderlondon/Shutterstock, (cleaning) Justinb/Fotolia, (Angler) Sabine Naumann/ tolia, (watching TV) Brian Jackson/Fotolia, (relaxing) Monkey Business/Fotolia; p. 116 (1) Paylessimages/Fotolia, (2) Tyler Olson/Fotolia, (3) Cohen/Ostrow/Photodisc/Getty Images, a) Duckman76/Fotolia, (4b) Duckman76/Fotolia, (5) Mc Xas/Fotolia, (6) Ryanking999/Fotolia, (7) Feng Yu/Shutterstock, (8) Claudia Paulussen/Fotolia; p. 118 (left) GL Archive/Alamy, ght) Ray Roberts/ Alamy; p. 119 (Miranda Lewis) Todd Keith/iStock/Thinkstock/Getty Images, (Miranda's house) Blend Images–JGI/Brand X Pictures/Getty Images, (Millerton ate Business College) Andres Rodriguez/Fotolia, (Miranda today) Andres Rodriguez/Fotolia; p. 120 (3a) Dmitry Pistrov/Fotolia, (3b) Qingwa/Fotolia, (4a) Paolo Bona/AGE Fotostock, o) Shutterbas/Fotolia, (5a) CandyBox Images/Fotolia, (5b) Uwimages/Fotolia; p. 121 (right) WaveBreakMediaMicro/Fotolia; p. 123 (1) Robert Kneschke/Shutterstock, (2) Auremar/ utterstock, (3) Jack Hollingsworth/Blend Images/Thinkstock/Getty Images, (4) Eurobanks/Shutterstock, (5) Ingram Publishing/Thinkstock/Getty Images, (6) Cameron Whitman/ ock/Thinkstock/Getty Images, (7) Francisco Romero/E+/Getty Images, (bottom right) JupiterImages/Stockbyte/Thinkstock/Getty Images; p. 125 (1) Arto/Fotolia, (2) Barbara Stitzer/ otoEdit, Inc., (3) Michael Jung/Fotolia, (4) Kzenon/Fotolia, (5) Minerva Studio/Fotolia, (6) Fuse/Thinkstock/Getty Images, (7) Kadmy/Fotolia, (8) AntonioDiaz/Fotolia, (9) Mangostock/ inkstock/Getty Images, (10) Bikeriderlondon/Fotolia, (11) Jeff Greenberg 4 of 6/Alamy, (12) Pressmaster/Fotolia, (13) Bill Bachmann/PhotoEdit, Inc., (14) Studiophotopro/Fotolia, 5) Tyler Olson/Fotolia, (16) Rob/Fotolia, (17) Rich Legg/E+/Getty Images; p. 126 (top left 1, 2) Arto/Fotolia, (top left 3) Jupiter Images/Stockbyte/Thinkstock/Getty Images, (top right 1) aveBreakMediaMicro/Fotolia, (top right 2) J.R. Bale/Alamy, (top right 3) Andres Rodriguez/Fotolia, (bottom 1) Michael Jung/Fotolia, (bottom 2) Dotshock/Shutterstock, (bottom 3) Sava exandru/E+/Getty Images, (bottom 4) Frillet Patrick /Hemis/Alamy, (bottom 5) Adisa/Fotolia, (bottom 6) DreamPictures/Blend Images/Alamy, (bottom 7) Bikeriderlondon/Shutterstock, ottom 8) Bertys30/Fotolia, (bottom 9) Omicron/Fotolia, (bottom 10) Eisenhans/Fotolia, (bottom 11) Jeremy Graham/DBimages/Alamy, (bottom 12) Bill Bachmann/PhotoEdit, Inc., ottom 13) ZUMA Press, Inc./Alamy (bottom 14) Marius Schwarz/Caro/Alamy; p. 127 (top 1) Radu Razvan/Fotolia, (top 2) Michael Jung/Fotolia, (top 3) Felix Mizioznikov/Shutterstock, p 4) Andrey Bandurenko/Fotolia, (bottom 1) Ken Scicluna/John Warburton-Lee Photography/Alamy, (bottom 2) Robbie Jack/Corbis, (bottom 3) India Images/Dinodia Photos/Alamy, ottom 4) Digital Vision/Getty Images, (bottom 5) Black 100/Allsport concepts/Getty Images, (bottom 6) Crashoran/Fotolia, (bottom 7) Glenn Harper/Alamy, (bottom 8) Agencyby/ ock/Thinkstock/Getty Images; p. 128 (1) Alexandra Karamyshev/Fotolia, Svetlana Ignatenko/Fotolia, (2) Michael Jung/Shutterstock, (3,4) Peter Atkins/Fotolia, (5) Ping han/Fotolia, Goodluz/Fotolia, (7) Venusangel/Fotolia, (8,9) JackF/Fotolia, (10) Olgavolodina/Fotolia, (11) Ariwasabi/Thinkstock/Getty Images, (12,13) Stuart Jenner/Shutterstock, (15) Dmitriy dkov/Fotolia, (16) Khvost/Fotolia, Littlestocker/Fotolia, (bottom) (1) Kastock/Fotolia, (2) JupiterImages/Thinkstock/Getty Images, (3) BananaStock/Thinkstock/Getty Images, Gina Sanders/Fotolia; p. 129 (1,2,3) RSnapshotPhotos/Shutterstock, (4) Red Chopsticks/Getty Images, (5) Cbckchristine/Fotolia, (6) Ignatius Wooster/Fotolia, (7,8,9) Celiafoto/Fotolia, ,11) Zoonar GmbH / Alamy, (12) Ilya Akinshin/Fotolia, (13) Tiler84/Fotolia, (14) Don Farrall/Getty Images,(15,16) Alexandr79/Fotolia, (17,18) Roman Samokhin/Fotolia, (19) Piotr winski/Fotolia, (20) MP2/Fotolia, (21,22) Womue/Fotolia, (23) Bonchan/Shutterstock, (24) Bruce Shippee/Fotolia, (25) Aleksandr Ugorenkov/Fotolia,(26) Andrey Kuzmin/Fotolia, ,28,29,30) Kornienko/Fotolia, (31,32,33,34) Food Collection/Getty Images, (35) 3dmentat/Fotolia, (36) HSN/Fotolia; p. 130 (top) (1) Soniccc/Fotolia, (2) Dianis Derics/Shutterstock, Danita Delimont/Alamy, (4) James Thew/Fotolia, (bottom) (1,2,3,4) Dennis MacDonald/Alamy; p. 131 (top) (1,2,3,8,9,10) Cynoclub/Fotolia, (4,5,6) Serghei Velusceac/Fotolia, (7) Ric lana Babor/Fotolia, (11) Mates/Fotolia, (12) Giuseppe Porzani/Fotolia, (13) Denlo109/Fotolia,(14) Fotomatrix/Fotolia, (15) Pieropoma/Fotolia,(bottom 1,2) Arti Zav/Fotolia, (3,4,5,14) icius Tupinamba/Fotolia, (6) Volf/Fotolia, (7) Natika/Fotolia, (8,9,10,11,12,13) Giuseppe Porzani/Fotolia,(15) Strannik72/Shutterstock, (16) Orlorl/Fotolia, (17,18) Popova Olga/Fotolia ; 132 (1) George Dolgikh/Fotolia, (2) Zvonimir Ore /Shutterstock, (3) Miravision/Fotolia, (4) Alexey Fursov /Shutterstock, (5) BlueOrange Studio /Shutterstock, (6) Vixit /Shutterstock, Lightpoet/Fotolia, (8) Dima266f/Fotolia, (face) Jaimie Duplass/Fotolia, (body) Edyta Pawlowska/Fotolia, (tongue) ArenaCreative/Fotolia; p. 133 (1) Sbarabu/Fotolia, (2) Scalaphotography/ tolia, (3) MUE/Fotolia, (4) Bota Horatiu/Fotolia, (5) Seen/Fotolia, (6) Klaus Eppele/Fotolia, (7) Eyetronic/Fotolia, (8) Dmitry Vereshchagin/Fotolia, (9) Jules Selmes/Dorling Kindersley, ., (10) Dispicture/Fotolia, (11) Klaus Eppele/Fotolia, (12) ReMuS/Fotolia; p. 134 (1) Dougal Waters/Getty Images, (2) Hill Street Studios/AGE Fotostock, (3) Radu Razvan/Fotolia, WavebreakMediaMicro/Fotolia, (5) BostjanT/E+/Getty Images, (6) Redsnapper/Alamy, (skiing) ARochau/Fotolia, (hiking) Maygutyak/Fotolia, (play) Mat Hayward/Fotolia, (garden) zoka303030/Fotolia, (curise) Frank Boston/Fotolia, (manicure) Mariiya/Fotolia; p. 144 (dress) Demidoff/Fotolia, (long skirt) PhotosIndia.com LLC/Alamy; p. 145 (suit) Elnur/Fotolia.

ustration credits: Kenneth Batelman pp. 37 (bottom-center), 61, 64, 65, 66, 120; John Ceballos pp. 48, 51, 95; Pascal Dejong pp. 11, 87; Karen Donnelly p. 111; Bob ucet p. 27; Len Ebert p. 110; Ingo Fast p. 21 (top); Scott Fray pp. 53, 80, 83; Brian Hughes pp. 22 (bottom), 25 (bottom), 36 (top), 89, 92; Robert Kemp p, 20; Jim Kopp p. 24; am Larkum p. 103; Pat Lewis p. 57 (right); Mona Mark p. 86; Robert McPhillips p. 119; Suzanne Morgensen p. 45 (bottom); Andy Myer pp. 7, 17; Sandy Nichols pp. 10, 37 (top), NSV Productions p. 37 (bottom-left, bottom-right); Dusan Petricic pp. 44, 45 (top), 60 (bottom), 72, 98, 100, 112; Phil Scheuer pp. 2, 54, 56, 57, 98, 99, 104 (top, top right), 106; l Stewart p. 36 (center-right); Don Stewart p. 48 (bottom); Gary Torrisi pp. 12, 25 (top), 68; Meryl Treatner pp. 37 (center), 110, 114; TSI Graphics pp. 21 (bottom), 46 (top right), (bottom); Anna Velfort pp. 12, 52, 76, 104, 106 (1-3 bottom); 108, 120 (bottom), 122; Patrick Welsh p. 71; XNR Productions pp. 36 (bottom), 60 (top).

xt credit: Page 86: Recipe for "Hungarian Cabbage and Noodles" by Rozanne Gold. Reprinted by permission.

LEARNING OBJECTIVES

Top Notch Fundamentals is designed for true beginning students or for students needing the suppo
of a very low-level beginning course. No prior knowledge of English is assumed or necessary.

	COMMUNICATION GOALS	VOCABULARY	GRAMMAR

UNIT 1
Names and Occupations
PAGE 4
	• Tell a classmate your occupation
	• Identify your classmates
	• Spell names
		• Occupations
		• The alphabet
		
		VOCABULARY BOOSTER
		• More occupations
			• Verb <u>be</u>:
			  ◦ Singular and plural statements, contractions
			  ◦ <u>Yes</u> / <u>no</u> questions and short answers
			  ◦ Common errors
			• Subject pronouns
			• Articles <u>a</u> / <u>an</u>
			• Nouns:
			  ◦ Singular and plural / Common and proper
			
			GRAMMAR BOOSTER Extra practice

UNIT 2 About People PAGE 12	• Introduce people • Tell someone your first and last name • Get someone's contact information	• Relationships (non-family) • Titles • First and last names • Numbers 0–20 VOCABULARY BOOSTER • More relationships / More titles	• Possessive nouns and adjectives • <u>Be from</u> / Questions with <u>Where</u>, common errors • Verb <u>be</u>: information questions with <u>What</u> GRAMMAR BOOSTER Extra practice
UNIT 3 Places and How to Get There PAGE 20	• Talk about locations • Discuss how to get places • Discuss transportation	• Places in the neighborhood • Locations • Ways to get places • Means of transportation • Destinations VOCABULARY BOOSTER • More places	• Verb <u>be</u>: questions with <u>Where</u> • Subject pronoun <u>it</u> • The imperative • <u>By</u> to express means of transportation GRAMMAR BOOSTER Extra practice

UNIT 4
Family
PAGE 28
	• Identify people in your family
	• Describe your relatives
	• Talk about your family
		• Family relationships
		• Adjectives to describe people
		• Numbers 21–101
		
		VOCABULARY BOOSTER
		• More adjectives
			• Verb <u>be</u>:
			  ◦ Questions with Who and common errors
			  ◦ With adjectives
			  ◦ Questions with <u>How old</u>
			• Adverbs <u>very</u> and <u>so</u>
			• Verb <u>have</u> / <u>has</u>: affirmative statements
			
			GRAMMAR BOOSTER Extra practice

UNIT 5 Events and Times PAGE 36	• Confirm that you're on time • Talk about the time of an event • Ask about birthdays	• What time is it? • <u>Early</u>, <u>on time</u>, <u>late</u> • Events • Days of the week • Ordinal numbers • Months of the year VOCABULARY BOOSTER • More events	• Verb <u>be</u>: questions about time • Prepositions <u>in</u>, <u>on</u>, and <u>at</u> for dates and times • Contractions and common errors GRAMMAR BOOSTER Extra practice

UNIT 6
Clothes
PAGE 44
	• Give and accept a compliment
	• Ask for colors and sizes
	• Describe clothes
		• Clothes
		• Colors and sizes
		• Opposite adjectives to describe clothes
		
		VOCABULARY BOOSTER
		• More clothes
			• Demonstratives <u>this</u>, <u>that</u>, <u>these</u>, <u>those</u>
			• The simple present tense: <u>like</u>, <u>want</u>, <u>need</u>, and <u>hav</u>
			  ◦ Affirmative and negative statements
			  ◦ Questions and short answers
			  ◦ Spelling rules and contractions
			• Adjective placement and common errors
			• <u>One</u> and <u>ones</u>
			
			GRAMMAR BOOSTER Extra practice

UNIT 7
Activities
PAGE 52
	• Talk about morning and evening activities
	• Describe what you do in your free time
	• Discuss household chores
		• Daily activities at home
		• Leisure activities
		• Household chores
		
		VOCABULARY BOOSTER
		• More household chores
			• The simple present tense:
			  ◦ Third-person singular spelling rules
			  ◦ Questions with <u>When</u> and <u>What time</u>
			  ◦ Questions with <u>How often</u>, time expressions
			  ◦ Questions with <u>Who</u> as subject, common errors
			• Frequency adverbs and time expressions:
			  ◦ Usage, placement, and common errors
			
			GRAMMAR BOOSTER Extra practice

Units 1–7 Review
PAGE 60

CONVERSATION STRATEGIES	LISTENING / PRONUNCIATION	READING / WRITING
Use <u>And you?</u> to show interest in another person Use <u>Excuse me</u> to initiate a conversation Use <u>Excuse me?</u> to indicate you haven't heard or didn't understand Use <u>Thanks!</u> to acknowledge someone's complying with a request	**Listening Tasks** • Circle the letter you hear • Identify correct spelling of names • Write the name you hear spelled • Identify the correct occupation • Write the missing information: names and occupations **Pronunciation** • Syllables	**Reading Text** • Simple forms and business cards **Writing Task** • Write affirmative and negative statements about people in a picture **WRITING BOOSTER** Guided writing practice
Identify someone's relationship to you when making an introduction Use <u>too</u> to reciprocate a greeting Begin a question with <u>And</u> to indicate you want additional information Repeat part of a question to clarify Repeat information to confirm	**Listening Tasks** • Complete statements about relationships • Circle the correct information • Fill in names, phone numbers, and e-mail addresses you hear **Pronunciation** • Stress in two-word pairs	**Reading Text** • Short descriptions of famous people, their occupations, and countries of origin **Writing Task** • Write sentences about your relationships **WRITING BOOSTER** Guided writing practice
Use <u>You're welcome</u> to formally acknowledge thanks Use <u>OK</u> to acknowledge advice Use <u>What about you?</u> to show interest in another person	**Listening Tasks** • Write the places you hear • Write the directions you hear, using affirmative and negative imperatives • Circle the means of transportation • Write <u>by</u> phrases, check destinations you hear **Pronunciation** • Falling intonation for questions with <u>Where</u>	**Reading Texts** • Simple maps and diagrams • Introductions of people, their relationships and occupations, where they live, and how they get to work **Writing Task** • Write questions and answers about the places in a complex picture **WRITING BOOSTER** Guided writing practice
Use <u>And</u> to shift the topic Use <u>Tell me about</u> to invite someone to talk about a topic Use <u>Well,</u> to indicate you are deciding how to begin a response Use <u>And how about?</u> to ask for more information Use <u>Really?</u> to show interest or mild surprise	**Listening Tasks** • Identify the picture of a relative being described • Choose the adjective that describes the people mentioned in a conversation **Pronunciation** • Number contrasts	**Reading Texts** • A family tree • A magazine article about famous actors and their families **Writing Task** • Write a description of the people in your family **WRITING BOOSTER** Guided writing practice
Use <u>Uh-oh</u> to indicate you may have made a mistake Use <u>Look</u> to focus someone's attention on something Use <u>Great!</u> to show enthusiasm for an idea Offer someone best wishes on his or her birthday Respond to a person's birthday wishes	**Listening Tasks** • Identify events and circle the correct times • Write the events you hear in a date book • Circle the dates you hear **Pronunciation** • Sentence rhythm	**Reading Texts** • A world map with time zones • Events posters • Newspaper announcements • A zodiac calendar **Writing Task** • Write about events at your school or in your city **WRITING BOOSTER** Guided writing practice
Acknowledge a compliment with <u>Thank you</u> Apologize with <u>I'm sorry</u> when expressing disappointing information Use <u>That's too bad</u> to express disappointment Use <u>What about you?</u> to ask for someone's opinion Use <u>Well</u> to soften a strong opinion	**Listening Tasks** • Confirm details about clothes • Determine colors of garments **Pronunciation** • Plural nouns	**Reading Texts** • A sales flyer from a department store **Writing Task** • Write sentences about the clothes you have, need, want, and like **WRITING BOOSTER** Guided writing practice
Say <u>Me?</u> to give yourself time to think of a personal response Use <u>Well</u> to introduce a lengthy response Use <u>What about you?</u> to ask for parallel information Use <u>So</u> to introduce a conversation topic Use <u>How about you?</u> to ask for parallel information Say <u>Sure</u> to indicate a willingness to answer Begin a response to an unexpected question with <u>Oh</u>	**Listening Task** • Match chores to the people who performed them **Pronunciation** • Third-person singular verb endings	**Reading Text** • A review of housekeeping robots **Writing Task** • Describe your typical week, using adverbs of frequency and time expressions **WRITING BOOSTER** Guided writing practice

	COMMUNICATION GOALS	VOCABULARY	GRAMMAR

UNIT 8
Home and Neighborhood
PAGE 64
	• Describe your neighborhood
	• Ask about someone's home
	• Talk about furniture and appliances
		• Buildings
		• Places in the neighborhood
		• Rooms
		• Furniture and appliances
		VOCABULARY BOOSTER
		• More home and office vocabulary
			• The simple present tense:
			  ◦ Questions with <u>Where</u>, prepositions of place
			• <u>There is</u> and <u>there are</u>:
			  ◦ Statements and <u>yes</u> / <u>no</u> questions
			  ◦ Contractions and common errors
			• Questions with <u>How many</u>
			GRAMMAR BOOSTER Extra practice

UNIT 9
Activities and Plans
PAGE 72
	• Describe today's weather
	• Discuss plans
	• Ask about people's activities
		• Weather expressions
		• Present and future time expressions
		VOCABULARY BOOSTER
		• More weather vocabulary / seasons
			• The present continuous:
			  ◦ Statements: form and usage
			  ◦ <u>Yes</u> / <u>no</u> questions
			  ◦ Information questions
			  ◦ For future plans
			• The present participle: spelling rules
			GRAMMAR BOOSTER Extra practice

UNIT 10 Food PAGE 80	• Discuss ingredients for a recipe • Offer and ask for foods • Invite someone to join you at the table	• Foods and drinks • Places to keep food in a kitchen • Containers and quantities • Cooking verbs **VOCABULARY BOOSTER** • More vegetables and fruits	• <u>How much</u> / <u>Are there any</u> • Count nouns and non-count nouns • <u>How much</u> / <u>Is there any</u> **GRAMMAR BOOSTER** Extra practice

UNIT 11
Past Events
PAGE 88
	• Tell someone about an event
	• Describe your past activities
	• Talk about your weekend
		• Past-time expressions
		• Outdoor activities
		VOCABULARY BOOSTER
		• More outdoor activities
			• The past tense of be; <u>There was</u> / <u>there were</u>:
			  ◦ Statements, questions, and contractions
			• The simple past tense
			  ◦ Regular verbs, irregular verbs
			  ◦ Statements, questions, and short answers
			GRAMMAR BOOSTER Extra practice

UNIT 12 Appearance and Health PAGE 96	• Describe appearance • Show concern about an injury • Suggest a remedy	• Adjectives to describe hair • The face • Parts of the body • Accidents and injuries • Ailments, remedies **VOCABULARY BOOSTER** • More parts of the body	• Describing people with <u>be</u> and <u>have</u> • <u>Should</u> + base form for suggestions **GRAMMAR BOOSTER** Extra practice
UNIT 13 Abilities and Requests PAGE 104	• Discuss your abilities • Politely decline an invitation • Ask for and agree to do a favor	• Abilities • Adverbs <u>well</u> and <u>badly</u> • Reasons for not doing something • Favors **VOCABULARY BOOSTER** • More musical instruments	• <u>Can</u> and <u>can't</u> for ability • <u>Too</u> + adjective, common errors • Polite requests with <u>Could you</u> + base form **GRAMMAR BOOSTER** Extra practice
UNIT 14 Life Events and Plans PAGE 112 Units 8–14 Review PAGE 120	• Get to know someone's life story • Discuss plans • Share your dreams for the future	• Some life events • Academic subjects • More leisure activities • Some dreams for the future **VOCABULARY BOOSTER** • More academic subjects • More leisure activities	• <u>Be going to</u> + base form **GRAMMAR BOOSTER** Extra practice

CONVERSATION STRATEGIES	LISTENING / PRONUNCIATION	READING / WRITING
Begin a question with And to indicate you want additional information Use Really? to introduce contradictory information Use Well to indicate you are deciding how to begin a response Respond positively to a description with Sounds nice! Use Actually to introduce an opinion that might surprise Say I don't know. I'm not sure to avoid making a direct negative statement	**Listening Tasks** • Determine the best house or apartment for clients of a real estate company • Complete statements about locations of furniture and appliances **Pronunciation** • Linking sounds	**Reading Texts** • House and apartment rental listings • Descriptions of people and their homes **Writing Task** • Compare and contrast your home with other homes **WRITING BOOSTER** Guided writing practice
Use Hi and Hey to greet people informally Say No kidding! to show surprise Use So to introduce a conversation topic Answer the phone with Hello? Identify yourself with This is on the phone Use Well, actually to begin an excuse Say Oh, I'm sorry after interrupting Say Talk to you later to indicate the end of a phone conversation	**Listening Tasks** • Determine weather and temperatures in cities in a weather report • Complete statements about people's activities, using the present continuous **Pronunciation** • Rising and falling intonation of yes / no and information questions	**Reading Texts** • A daily planner • The weather forecast for four cities **Writing Task** • Write about plans for the week, using the present continuous **WRITING BOOSTER** Guided writing practice
Say I'll check to indicate you'll get information for someone Decline an offer politely with No, thanks Use Please pass the to ask for something at the table Say Here you go as you offer something Say Nice to see you to greet someone you already know Use You too to repeat a greeting politely	**Listening Task** • Identify the foods discussed in conversations **Pronunciation** • Vowel sounds: /i/, /ɪ/, /eɪ/, /ɛ/, /æ/	**Reading Texts** • Recipe cards • A weekly schedule **Writing Task** • Write about what you eat in a typical day **WRITING BOOSTER** Guided writing practice
Ask Why? to ask for a clearer explanation Use What about? to ask for more information Use a double question to clarify Use just to minimize the importance of an action Say Let me think to gain time to answer Say Oh yeah to indicate you just remembered something	**Listening Tasks** • Circle the year you hear • Infer the correct day or month • Choose activities mentioned in conversations **Pronunciation** • Simple past tense regular verb endings	**Reading Text** • A blog in which people describe what they did the previous weekend **Writing Task** • Write about the activities of two people, based on a complex picture • Write about your weekend and what you did **WRITING BOOSTER** Guided writing practice
Use Oh to indicate you've understood Say No kidding to show surprise Say I'm sorry to hear that, Oh, no, and That's too bad to express sympathy Use Actually to introduce an opinion that might surprise Use What's wrong? to ask about an illness Use really to intensify advice with should Respond to good advice with Good idea Say I hope you feel better when someone feels sick	**Listening Tasks** • Identify the people described in conversations • Complete statements about injuries • Identify the ailments and remedies suggested in conversations **Pronunciation** • More vowel sounds	**Reading Text** • A magazine article about two celebrities **Writing Task** • Write a description of someone you know **WRITING BOOSTER** Guided writing practice
Use Actually to give information Use Really? to show surprise or interest Suggest a shared course of action with Let's Politely decline a suggestion with I'm really sorry but and a reason Accept a refusal with Maybe some other time Use Sure and No problem to agree to someone's request for a favor	**Listening Task** • Complete requests for favors **Pronunciation** • Blending of sounds: Could you	**Reading Text** • An article about infant-toddler development **Writing Task** • Describe things people can and can't do when they get old **WRITING BOOSTER** Guided writing practice
Use And you? to show interest in another person Use Not really to soften a negative response Ask What about you? to extend the conversation Use Well and Actually to explain or clarify	**Listening Tasks** • Choose correct statements • Circle correct words or phrases • Complete statements about activities, using the present continuous • Infer people's wishes for the future **Pronunciation** • Diphthongs	**Reading Text** • A short biography of Harry Houdini **Writing Task** • Write your own illustrated life story, including plans and dreams for the future **WRITING BOOSTER** Guided writing practice

riting Booster . . . . page 146   *Top Notch Pop* Lyrics . . . . page 150

vii

TO THE TEACHER

What is *Top Notch?*
Top Notch is a six-level* communicative course that prepares adults and young adults to interact successfully and confidently with both native and non-native speakers of English.

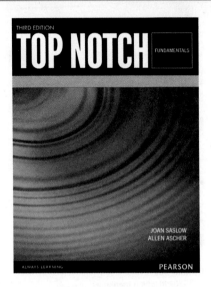

The goal of *Top Notch* is to make English unforgettable through:
- Multiple exposures to new language
- Numerous opportunities to practice it
- Deliberate and intensive recycling

The *Top Notch* course has two beginning levels—*Top Notch Fundamentals* for true beginners and *Top Notch 1* for false beginners. *Top Notch* is benchmarked to the Global Scale of English and is tightly correlated to the Can-do Statements of the Common European Framework of Reference.

Each full level of *Top Notch* contains material for 60–90 hours of classroom instruction. In addition, the entire course can be tailored to blended learning with an integrated online component, *MyEnglishLab*.

NEW This third edition of *Top Notch* includes these new features: Extra Grammar Exercises, digital full-color Vocabulary Flash Cards, Conversation Activator videos, Pronunciation Coach videos, and a Writing Booster.

* *Summit 1* and *Summit 2* are the titles of the 5th and 6th levels of the *Top Notch* course.

Award-Winning Instructional Design*

Daily confirmation of progress
Each easy-to-follow two-page lesson begins with a clearly stated practical communication goal closely aligned to the Common European Framework's Can-do Statements. All activities are integrated with the goal, giving vocabulary and grammar meaning and purpose. *Now You Can* activities ensure that students achieve each goal and confirm their progress in every class session.

True-beginner vocabulary and grammar
Clear captioned picture-dictionary illustrations with accompanying audio take the guesswork out of meaning and pronunciation. Grammar presentations clarify form, meaning, and use. The unique *Recycle this Language* feature continually puts known words and grammar in front of students' eyes as they communicate, to make sure language remains active. A new Writing Booster in the back of the Student's Book provides guided writing practice that incorporates vocabulary and grammar from the unit.

Authentic social language
Even beginning students should learn appealing natural social language. Forty-two memorable Conversation Models provide lively controlled conversation practice that ensures enthusiasm and motivation.

Active listening syllabus
All Vocabulary presentations, Pronunciation presentations, Conversation Models, Listening Comprehension exercises, and Readings are recorded on the audio, ensuring that students develop good pronunciation, intonation, and auditory memory. In addition, approximately fifty tasks specifically developed for beginning learners develop fundamental comprehension skills.

We wish you and your students enjoyment and success with *Top Notch Fundamentals*. We wrote it for you.

Joan Saslow and Allen Ascher

* *Top Notch* is the recipient of the Association of Educational Publishers' *Distinguished Achievement Award*.

viii

ActiveTeach

Maximize the impact of your *Top Notch* lessons. This digital tool provides an interactive classroom experience that can be used with or without an interactive whiteboard (IWB). It includes a full array of digital and printable features.

For class presentation . . .

- **NEW** Conversation Activator videos: increase students' confidence in oral communication
- **NEW** Pronunciation Coach videos: facilitate clear and fluent oral expression
- **NEW** Extra Grammar Exercises: ensure mastery of grammar
- **NEW** Digital Full-Color Vocabulary Flash Cards: accelerate retention of new vocabulary

PLUS

- Clickable Audio: instant access to the complete classroom audio program
- *Top Notch TV* Video Program: a hilarious sitcom and authentic on-the-street interviews
- *Top Notch Pop* Songs and Karaoke: original songs for additional language practice

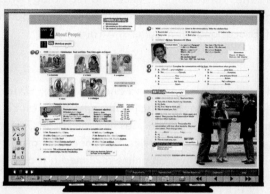

For planning . . .

- A *Methods Handbook* for a communicative classroom
- Detailed timed lesson plans for each two-page lesson
- *Top Notch TV* teaching notes
- Complete answer keys, audio scripts, and video scripts

For extra support . . .

- Hundreds of extra printable activities, with teaching notes
- *Top Notch Pop* language exercises
- *Top Notch TV* activity worksheets

For assessment . . .

- Ready-made unit and review achievement tests with options to edit, add, or delete items.

MyEnglishLab

An optional online learning tool

- **NEW** Grammar Coach videos plus the Pronunciation Coach videos, and Digital Vocabulary Flash Cards
- **NEW** Immediate meaningful feedback on wrong answers
- **NEW** Remedial grammar exercises
- Interactive practice of all material presented in the course
- Grade reports that display performance and time on task
- Auto-graded achievement tests

Workbook

Lesson-by-lesson written exercises to accompany the Student's Book

Full-Course Placement Tests

Choose printable or online version

Classroom Audio Program

- A set of Audio CDs, as an alternative to the clickable audio in the ActiveTeach
- Contains a variety of authentic regional and non-native accents to build comprehension of diverse English speakers
- **NEW** The entire audio program is available for students at www.english.com/topnotch3e. The mobile app *Top Notch Go* allows access anytime, anywhere and lets students practice at their own pace.

Teacher's Edition and Lesson Planner

- Detailed interleaved lesson plans, language and culture notes, answer keys, and more
- Also accessible in digital form in the ActiveTeach

For more information: www.pearsonelt.com/topnotch3e

ABOUT THE AUTHORS

Joan Saslow

Joan Saslow has taught in a variety of programs in South America and the United States. She is author or coauthor of a number of widely used courses, some of which are *Ready to Go*, *Workplace Plus*, *Literacy Plus*, and *Summit*. She is also author of *English in Context*, a series for reading science and technology. Ms. Saslow was the series director of *True Colors* and *True Voices*. She has participated in the English Language Specialist Program in the U.S. Department of State's Bureau of Educational and Cultural Affairs.

Allen Ascher

Allen Ascher has been a teacher and teacher trainer in China and the United States, as well as academic director of the intensive English program at Hunter College. Mr. Ascher has also been an ELT publisher and was responsible for publication and expansion of numerous well-known courses including *True Colors*, *NorthStar*, the *Longman TOEFL Preparation Series*, and the *Longman Academic Writing Series*. He is coauthor of *Summit* and he wrote the "Teaching Speaking" module of *Teacher Development Interactive*, an online multimedia teacher-training program.

Ms. Saslow and Mr. Ascher are frequent presenters at professional conferences and have been coauthoring courses for teens, adults, and young adults since 2002.

AUTHORS' ACKNOWLEDGMENTS

The authors are indebted to these reviewers, who provided extensive and detailed feedback and suggestions for *Top Notch*, as well as the hundreds of teachers who completed surveys and participated in groups.

Manuel Wilson Alvarado Miles, Quito, Ecuador • **Shirley Ando**, Otemae University, Hyogo, Japan • **Vanessa de Andrade**, CCBEU Inter Americano, Curitiba, Brazil • **Miguel Arrazola**, CBA, Santa Cruz, Bolivia • **Mark Barta**, Proficiency School of English, São Paulo, Brazil • **Edwin Bello**, PROULEX, Guadalajara, Mexico • **Mary Blum**, CBA, Cochabamba, Bolivia • **María Elizabeth Boccia**, Proficiency School of English, São Paulo, Brazil • **Pamela Cristina Borja Baltán**, Quito, Ecuador • **Eliana Anabel L. Buccia**, AMICANA, Mendoza, Argentina • **José Humberto Calderón Díaz**, CALUSAC, Guatemala City, Guatemala • **María Teresa Calienes Csirke**, Idiomas Católica, Lima, Peru • **Esther María Carbo Morales**, Quito, Ecuador • **Jorge Washington Cárdenas Castillo**, Quito, Ecuador • **Eréndira Yadira Carrera García**, UVM Chapultepec, Mexico City, Mexico • **Viviane de Cássia Santos Carlini**, Spectrum Line, Pouso Alegre, Brazil • **Centro Colombo Americano**, Bogota, Colombia • **Guven Ciftci**, Fatih University, Istanbul, Turkey • **Diego Cisneros**, CBA, Tarija, Bolivia • **Paul Crook**, Meisei University, Tokyo, Japan • **Alejandra Díaz Loo**, El Cultural, Arequipa, Peru • **Jesús G. Díaz Osío**, Florida National College, Miami, USA • **María Eid Ceneviva**, CBA, Bolivia • **Amalia Elvira Rodríguez Espinoza De Los Monteros**, Guayaquil, Ecuador • **María Argelia Estrada Vásquez**, CALUSAC, Guatemala City, Guatemala • **John Fieldeldy**, College of Engineering, Nihon University, Aizuwakamatsu-shi, Japan • **Marleni Humbelina Flores Urízar**, CALUSAC, Guatemala City, Guatemala • **Gonzalo Fortune**, CBA, Sucre, Bolivia • **Andrea Fredricks**, Embassy CES, San Francisco, USA • **Irma Gallegos Peláez**, UVM Tlalpan, Mexico City, Mexico • **Alberto Gamarra**, CBA, Santa Cruz, Bolivia • **María Amparo García Peña**, ICPNA Cusco, Peru • **Amanda Gillis-Furutaka**, Kyoto Sangyo University, Kyoto, Japan • **Martha Angelina González Párraga**, Guayaquil, Ecuador • **Octavio Gorduno Ruiz** • **Ralph Grayson**, Idiomas Católica, Lima, Peru • **Murat Gultekin**, Fatih University, Istanbul, Turkey • **Oswaldo Gutiérrez**, PROULEX, Guadalajara, Mexico • **Ayaka Hashinishi**, Otemae University, Hyogo, Japan • **Alma Lorena Hernández de Armas**, CALUSAC, Guatemala City, Guatemala • **Kent Hill**, Seigakuin University, Saitama-ken, Japan • **Kayoko Hirao**, Nichii Gakkan Company, COCO Juku, Japan • **Jesse Huang**, National Central University, Taoyuan, Taiwan • **Eric Charles Jones**, Seoul University of Technology, Seoul, South Korea • **Jun-Chen Kuo**, Tajen University, Pingtung , Taiwan • **Susan Krieger**, Embassy CES, San Francisco, USA • **Ana María de la Torre Ugarte**, ICPNA Chiclayo, Peru • **Erin Lemaistre**, Chung-Ang University, Seoul, South Korea • **Eleanor S. Leu**, Soochow University, Taipei, Taiwan • **Yihui Li (Stella Li)**, Fooyin University, Kaohsiung, Taiwan • **Chin-Fan Lin**, Shih Hsin University, Taipei, Taiwan • **Linda Lin**, Tatung Institute of Technology, Taiwan • **Kristen Lindblom**, Embassy CES, San Francisco, USA • **Patricio David López Logacho**, Quito, Ecuador • **Diego López Tasara**, Idiomas Católica, Lima, Peru • **Neil Macleod**, Kansai Gaidai University, Osaka, Japan • **Adriana Marcés**, Idiomas Católica, Lima, Peru • **Robyn McMurray**, Pusan National University, Busan, South Korea • **Paula Medina**, London Language Institute, London, Canada • **Juan Carlos Muñoz**, American School Way, Bogota, Colombia • **Noriko Mori**, Otemae University, Hyogo, Japan • **Adrián Esteban Narváez Pacheco**, Cuenca, Ecuador • **Tim Newfields**, Tokyo University Faculty of Economics, Tokyo, Japan • **Ana Cristina Ochoa**, CCBEU Inter Americano, Curitiba, Brazil • **Tania Elizabeth Ortega Santacruz**, Cuenca, Ecuador • **Martha Patricia Páez**, Quito, Ecuador • **María de Lourdes Pérez Valdespino**, Universidad del Valle de México, Mexico • **Wahrena Elizabeth Pfeister**, University of Suwon, Gyeonggi-Do, South Korea • **Wayne Allen Pfeister**, University of Suwon, Gyeonggi-Do, South Korea • **Andrea Rebonato**, CCBEU Inter Americano, Curitiba, Brazil • **Thoma Robb**, Kyoto Sangyo University, Kyoto, Japan • **Mehran Sabet**, Seigakuin University, Saitama-ken, Japan • **Majid Safadaran Mosazadeh**, ICPNA Chiclayo, Peru • **Timothy Samuelson**, BridgeEnglish, Denver, USA • **Héctor Sánchez**, PROULEX, Guadalajara, Mexico • **Mónica Alexandra Sánchez Escalante**, Quito, Ecuado • **Jorge Mauricio Sánchez Montalván**, Quito, Universidad Politécnica Salesiana (UPS), Ecuador • **Letícia Santos**, ICBEU Ibiá, Brazil • **Elena Sapp**, INTO Oregon State University, Corvallis, USA • **Robert Sheridan**, Otemae University, Hyogo, Japan • **John Eric Sherman**, Hong Ik University Seoul, South Korea • **Brooks Slaybaugh**, Asia University, Tokyo, Japan • **João Vitor Soares**, NACC, São Paulo, Brazil • **Silvia Solares**, CBA, Sucre, Bolivia • **Chayawan Sonchaeng**, Delaw County Community College, Media, PA • **María Julia Suárez**, CBA, Cochabamba, Bolivia • **Ele Sudakova**, English Language Center, Kiev, Ukra • **Richard Swingle**, Kansai Gaidai College, Osa Japan • **Blanca Luz Terrazas Zamora**, ICPNA Cusco, Peru • **Sandrine Ting**, St. John's Universit New Taipei City, Taiwan • **Christian Juan Torre Medina**, Guayaquil, Ecuador • **Raquel Torrico** CBA, Sucre, Bolivia • **Jessica Ueno**, Otemae University, Hyogo, Japan • **Ximena Vacaflor C** CBA, Tarija, Bolivia • **René Valdivia Pereira**, C Santa Cruz, Bolivia • **Solange Lopes Vinagre Costa**, SENAC, São Paulo, Brazil • **Magno Alejandro Vivar Hurtado**, Cuenca, Ecuador • **Dr. Wen-hsien Yang**, National Kaohsiung Hospitality College, Kaohsiung, Taiwan • **Juan Zárate**, El Cultural, Arequipa, Peru

Welcome to *Top Notch*!

GOAL Introduce yourself

▶1:02 CONVERSATION MODEL Read and listen.

A: Hi. I'm Martin.
B: Hi, Martin. I'm Ben.

A: Nice to meet you, Ben.
B: Nice to meet you, too.

▶1:03 RHYTHM AND INTONATION Listen again and repeat. Then practice the Conversation Model with a partner.

NOW YOU CAN Introduce yourself

PAIR WORK Now introduce yourself to your classmates.

▶1:04 **Greetings**
Hi.
Hello.
I'm [Lisa].

▶1:05 **Responses**
Nice to meet you.
Glad to meet you.
It's a pleasure to meet you.

1 ▶1:06 **CONVERSATION MODEL** Read and listen.

A: Hi, Len. How are you?
B: Fine, thanks. And you?
A: I'm fine.

2 ▶1:07 **RHYTHM AND INTONATION** Listen again and repeat. Then practice the Conversation Model with a partner.

3 ▶1:08 **VOCABULARY** • *More greetings* Read and listen. Then listen again and repeat.

1 Good morning. 8:00 A.M.

2 Good afternoon. 2:00 P.M.

3 Good evening. 6:00 P...

NOW YOU CAN Greet people

PAIR WORK Now greet your classmates.

▶1:09 **Greetings**
How are you?
How's everything?
How's it going?

▶1:10 **Responses**
☺ Fine. / I'm fine.
   Great.
😐 Not bad.
   So-so.

▶1:11 CONVERSATION MODEL Read and listen.

A: Good-bye, Charlotte.
B: Good-bye, Emily.
A: See you tomorrow.
B: OK. See you!

▶1:12 RHYTHM AND INTONATION Listen again
and repeat. Then practice the Conversation
Model with a partner.

NOW YOU CAN **Say good-bye**

PAIR WORK Now say good-bye to your classmates.

▶1:13 **Ways to say good-bye**
Good-bye.
Bye.
See you later.
Take care.

NOW I CAN

☒ Introduce myself.
☐ Greet people.
☐ Say good-bye.

COMMUNICATION GOALS
1 Tell a classmate your occupation.
2 Identify your classmates.
3 Spell names.

UNIT 1 Names and Occupations

LESSON 1 **GOAL** Tell a classmate your occupation

VOCABULARY BOOSTER
More occupations • p. 125

1 ▶1:14 **VOCABULARY** • *Occupations* Read and listen. Then listen again and repeat.

1 a teacher

2 a student

3 an architect

4 an actor

5 an athlete

6 a musician

7 an artist

8 a banker

9 a singer

10 a flight attendant

2 **PAIR WORK** Say the name of an occupation. Your partner points (☞) to the picture.

3 **GRAMMAR** • *Verb be: singular statements / Contractions*

Affirmative statements / Contractions	Negative statements / Contractions
I am Ann. / I'm Ann.	I am not Jen. / I'm not Jen.
You are an architect. / You're an architect.	You are not an artist. / You're not an artist. / You aren't an artist.
He is a teacher. / He's a teacher.	He is not a student. / He's not a student. / He isn't a student.
She is a singer. / She's a singer.	She is not a banker. / She's not a banker. / She isn't a banker.

Articles a / an
a teacher
an actor

GRAMMAR PRACTICE Write the article <u>a</u> or <u>an</u> for each occupation.

1 I'm ..an.. architect.
2 She's ..a.. student.
3 He's not ..a.. banker.
4 He is ..a.. musician.
5 She is ..a.. singer.
6 I'm not ..an.. athlete.

PAIR WORK Point to the people on page 4. Say *He's* _____ or *She's* _____.

❝ He's a teacher. ❞

❝ She's a flight attendant. ❞

VOCABULARY / GRAMMAR PRACTICE Read the names and occupations. Write affirmative and negative statements.

Orlando Bloom | actor

LUIS MIGUEL
SINGER

musician

Joo Yeon Sir

Marta
ATHLETE

1 Orlando Bloom ..*is an actor. He's not a singer.*..
2 Luis Miguel ..*is a Singer. He's not an actor*..
3 Joo Yeon Sir ..*is a musician. She is not an athlete*..
4 Marta ..*is an Athlete. She is not a musician*..

NOW YOU CAN Tell a classmate your occupation

▶1:15 **CONVERSATION MODEL** Read and listen.

A: What do you do?
B: I'm an architect. And you?
A: I'm a banker.

▶1:16 **RHYTHM AND INTONATION** Listen again and repeat. Then practice the Conversation Model with a partner.

CONVERSATION ACTIVATOR With a partner, personalize the conversation. Use your own occupations.

A: What do you do?
B: I'm a doctor. And you?
A: I'm a house wife

CHANGE PARTNERS Tell another classmate your occupation.

5

GOAL Identify your classmates

1 ▶ 1:17 VOCABULARY • *More occupations* Read and listen. Then listen again and repeat.

1 She's **a chef**.

2 He's **a writer**.
(aydır (yazar)

3 She's **a manager**.

4 She's **a scientist**.
Bilimadamı

5 He's **a doctor**.

6 She's **an engineer**.
(mühendis)

7 He's **a photographer**.

8 He's **a pilot**.
pəylət

2 GRAMMAR • *Singular and plural nouns /* <u>Be</u>: *plural statements*

Singular nouns	Plural nouns
a chef	2 chefs
an athlete	3 athletes

Subject pronouns	
Singular	**Plural**
I	we
you	you
he	they
she	

Affirmative statements / Contractions

We **are** photographers. / We're photographers.
You **are** scientists. / You're scientists.
They **are** writers. / They're writers.

Negative statements / Contractions

We **are not** chefs. / We're not chefs. / We **aren't** chefs.
You **are not** pilots. / You're not pilots. / You **aren't** pilots.
They **are not** artists. / They're not artists. / They **aren't** artists.

3 GRAMMAR PRACTICE Complete each statement with a singular or plural form of <u>be</u>.

1 I **'m** a writer.
2 She **'s** not a pilot.
3 We **are** doctors.
4 They **are** not scientists.
5 We **are** managers.

4 VOCABULARY / GRAMMAR PRACTICE Circle the correct word or words to complete each statement.

1 I am (**an artist** / artists / artist).
2 We are (a flight attendant / **flight attendants** / flight attendant).
3 She is (banker / **a banker** / bankers).
4 They are (a writer / **writers** / writer).

Goguller

GRAMMAR • Be: yes / no questions and short answers

Yes / no questions		Short answers				
Are you		Yes, I **am**.			No, I'm not.	
Is he	an architect?	Yes,	he / she	is.	No,	he's / she's	not.
Is Tanya						
Are you						
Are they	musicians?	Yes,	we / they	are.	No,	we're / they're	not.
Are Ted and Jane						

Be careful!

Yes, I am.	NOT	Yes, I'm.
Yes, she is.	NOT	Yes, she's.
Yes, we are.	NOT	Yes, we're.

GRAMMAR PRACTICE Complete the conversations. Use contractions when possible.

1 A: ...*Are*.... they Abby and Jonah?
   B: Yes, ...*they are*.. .

2 A: ..*Is*........ Hanna a scientist?
   B: No, she'.....*Is not. She is* a doctor.

3 A: ..*are*...... you Rachel and Philip?
   B: No, we'....*are....not.* ...*We are*..Judith and Jack.

4 A: ..*are you* a chef?
   B: Yes, I'*m*.................. .

5 A: ..*Is*............ he Evan?
   B: No, *he is*........ not. He'.*is*.... Michael.

6 A: ..*Is*.... Tim an actor?
   B: No, he'..*is not. he is*.. a teacher.

PAIR WORK Practice the conversations from Exercise 6.

PAIR WORK Ask your partner two questions. Answer your partner's questions.

" Are you an artist? "

" Yes, I am. "

OW YOU CAN Identify your classmates

▶1:18 **CONVERSATION MODEL** Read and listen.

A: Excuse me. Are you Marie?
B: No, I'm not. I'm Laura. That's Marie.
A: Where?
B: Right over there.
A: Thank you.
B: You're welcome.

▶1:19 **RHYTHM AND INTONATION** Listen again and repeat. Then practice the Conversation Model with a partner.

CONVERSATION ACTIVATOR With a partner, personalize the conversation. Use real names. Then change roles.

A: Excuse me. Are you .... ?
B: No, I'm not. I'm .... That's ....
A: Where?
B: Right over there.
A: Thank you.
B: You're welcome.

CHANGE PARTNERS Identify other classmates.

LESSON 3 GOAL Spell names

DIGITAL FLASH CARDS

1 ▶1:20 **VOCABULARY • *The alphabet*** Read and listen. Then listen again and repeat.

A B C D E F G H I J K L M

N O P Q R S T U V W X Y Z

2 ▶1:21 **LISTENING COMPREHENSION** Listen. Circle the letter you hear.

1 A K	4 U O	7 F X	10 J G	13 D G
2 B E	5 B Z	8 X S	11 L N	14 H K
3 M N	6 T C	9 Z V	12 K J	15 P E

3 **PAIR WORK** Read 10 letters aloud to your partner. Point to the letters you hear.

N M W

J C I Y

F Q O E P D

H B S Z R K

V U L G

A T X

4 ▶1:22 **LISTENING COMPREHENSION** Listen. Circle the correct spelling. Then spell each name aloud.

1	Green	Greene	Grin
2	Leigh	Lee	Li
3	Katharine	Katherine	Catharine

5 ▶1:23 **LISTENING COMPREHENSION** Listen to the conversations. Write the names.

1 ....

2 ....

3 ....

6 **GRAMMAR • *Proper nouns and common nouns***

Proper nouns
The names of people and places are proper nouns. Use a capital letter to begin a proper noun.
Melanie Pepper New Delhi Nicaragua

Common nouns
Other nouns are common nouns. Use a lowercase letter to begin a common noun.
morning doctor student

Capital letters
A B C
Lowercase letters
a b c

7 GRAMMAR PRACTICE Circle the proper nouns. Underline the common nouns.

1 Mary Chase   *özel isim*   **3** name   *cins isim*   **5** partners

2 letter   **4** France   **6** alphabet

8 GRAMMAR PRACTICE Check ☑ the common nouns. Capitalize the proper nouns.

☐ **1** marie   ☐ **3** sarah browne   ☐ **5** canada   ☐ **7** letter

☑ **2** partner   ☐ **4** teacher   ☐ **6** noun   ☐ **8** grammar

9 ▶1:24 **PRONUNCIATION • Syllables** Read and listen. Then listen again and repeat.

1 syllable	**2 syllables**	**3 syllables**	**4 syllables**
chef	bank • er	ar • chi • tect	pho • tog • ra • pher

0 ▶1:25 **PAIR WORK** First, take turns saying each word. Write the number of syllables. Then listen to check your work.

1 teacher ....   **3** vocabulary ....   **5** occupation ....

2 students ....   **4** alphabet ....   **6** they're ....

NOW YOU CAN   Spell names

▶1:26 **CONVERSATION MODEL** Read and listen.

A: Hello. I'm John Bello.
B: Excuse me?
A: John Bello.
B: How do you spell that?
A: B-E-L-L-O.
B: Thanks!

▶1:27 **RHYTHM AND INTONATION**
Listen again and repeat. Then
practice the Conversation
Model with a partner.

CONVERSATION ACTIVATOR
With a partner, personalize the
conversation. Use real names.
Then change roles.

A: Hello. I'm ...Rukiye
B: Excuse me?
A: Rukiye Bayam
B: How do you spell that?
A: B.A.Y.A.M
B: Thanks!   **DON'T STOP!**

> **Ask about occupations:**
> What do you do?

CHANGE PARTNERS
Personalize the conversation again.

EXTENSION

1 ▶1:28 **LISTENING COMPREHENSION** Listen to the conversations. Write the number of each conversation in the correct box.

 □
 □
 □
 □

2 ▶1:29 **LISTENING COMPREHENSION** Listen to the conversations. Complete the information.

NAME	OCCUPATION
Porter	

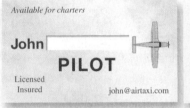

Available for charters
John _____
PILOT
Licensed
Insured   john@airtaxi.com

World Language Institute
Lorraine Clare   1-800-555-6788
English _____

3 **PAIR WORK** Choose a famous person. Write that person's information on the form. Then play the role of that person and introduce "yourself" to your partner.

NAME:
OCCUPATION:

❝ Hi. I'm [Bradley Cooper]. I'm [an actor]. And you? ❞

4 **VOCABULARY / GRAMMAR PRACTICE** Answer the questions about four famous people. Use subject pronouns and contractions.

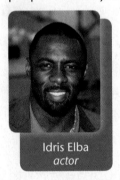
Idris Elba
actor

Paulina Aguirre
singer

Zheng Jie
athlete

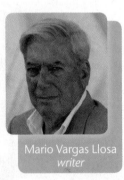
Mario Vargas Llosa
writer

1 Is Idris Elba an actor or a singer?
He's an actor.

2 Is Paulina Aguirre a singer?
yes she is a singer

3 Is Zheng Jie a teacher?
no she isn't a teacher

4 Are Zheng Jie and Mario Vargas Llosa scientists?
No they aren't a scientists

5 Is Mario Vargas Llosa an actor?
no. He's not a write

6 Is Zheng Jie an athlete or a writer?
She's an athlete

5 **PERSONAL RESPONSES** Write responses with real information.

1 "Hi. I'm Art Potter."
(YOU) _Hi. I'm Putin._

2 "Are you a teacher?"
(YOU) _no. I'm not a teacher_
I'm a student

3 "What do you do?"
(YOU) _I'm a doctor._

4 "Thank you."
(YOU) _Thank you._
You're welcome

GRAMMAR BOOSTE
Unit 1 review • p. 135

For additional language practice . . .

♫ **TOP NOTCH** POP • Lyrics p. 1!
"What Do You Do?"

DIGITAL SONG	DIGITAL KARAOKE

R-O-S-E

Rose

POINT Name the occupations in the pictures. For example:

She's an artist.

PAIR WORK

1 Ask and answer questions about the people. For example:

Is John a photographer? Yes, he is.

2 Create conversations for the people. For example:

Hi. I'm ___.

WRITING Write affirmative and negative statements about the people in the picture. For example:

Rose is an artist. She's not an architect.

WRITING BOOSTER p. 146
Guidance for this writing exercise

John
Ben
Matt
Tim
Martin
Marie
Ann
Emily

✓ **NOW I CAN**

☐ Tell a classmate my occupation.
☐ Identify my classmates.
☐ Spell names.

COMMUNICATION GOALS
1 Introduce people.
2 Tell someone your first and last name.
3 Get someone's contact information.

UNIT 2 About People

LESSON 1 GOAL Introduce people

1 ▶1:32 **VOCABULARY • *Relationships*** Read and listen. Then listen again and repeat.

1 a classmate *sınıf arkadaşı*

2 a friend *Arkadaş*

3 a neighbor *komşu*

4 a boss *patron*

5 a colleague *iş arkadaşı*

VOCABULARY BOOSTER
More relationships • p. 126

2 **GRAMMAR • *Possessive nouns and adjectives***

Ms. Ellis is **Joe's** teacher.
Joe is **her** student.

Possessive nouns
Al Smith is **Kate's** boss.
Larry's colleague is Teresa.
We are **Sara and Todd's** neighbors.
I am **Ms. Tan's** student.
We are **Marty's** classmates.

Possessive adjectives
He is **her** boss.
Teresa is **his** colleague.
We are **their** neighbors.
She is **my** teacher.
Marty is **our** classmate.

Subject pronouns		Possessive adjectives
I	→	my
you	→	your
he	→	his
she	→	her
we	→	our
they	→	their

3 **GRAMMAR PRACTICE** Circle the correct word or words to complete each sentence.

1 Mr. Thomas is (<u>my</u> / I) boss.
2 Is Mrs. Cory (you / <u>your</u>) teacher?
3 Is (<u>she</u> / her) Dr. Kim?
4 Are (<u>they</u> / their) Connie and Sam?
5 Are (your / <u>you</u>) Barry's friend?

6 He's (<u>my</u> / I) colleague.
7 Mr. Benson is (Alec / <u>Alec's</u>) neighbor.
8 Jake is (Ms. Rose / Ms. <u>Rose's</u>) student.
9 (<u>He's</u> / His) an architect.
10 (Kyle / <u>Kyle's</u>) and Ray's classmate is Gail.

4 **PAIR WORK** Tell a classmate about at least three of your relationships. Use the Vocabulary.

> " Jerry is my classmate. Ted and Jan Keyes are my neighbors. "

▶1:33 **LISTENING COMPREHENSION** Listen to the conversations. Write the relationships.

1 Bruce is her ....   **3** Mr. Grant is her ....   **5** Carlos is his ....

2 Patty is his ....   **4** Rob is her ....

GRAMMAR • _Be from_ / Questions with _Where_

I'm from Miami.

Are you from Paraguay?   Yes, I am. / No, I'm not.
Is she from Moscow?   Yes, she is. / No, she's not.

Where are you from?   We're from Bangkok.
Where's she from?   She's from Canada.

Be careful!
Are you from Spain?
Yes, I am. NOT Yes, ~~I am from~~.

Contractions
Where is → **Where's**
Where are NOT ~~Where're~~

GRAMMAR PRACTICE Complete the conversations with _be from_. Use contractions when possible.

1 A: ..Where's.. your neighbor .... ?
 B: She .... Canada.

2 A: .... they .... ?
 B: .... Paris.

3 A: .... Mr. Tanaka .... ?
 B: .... Japan.

4 A: .... your boss .... ?
 B: He .... Fortaleza.

5 A: .... you and your friend .... ?
 B: .... Busan.

6 A: .... Pat's colleagues .... ?
 B: .... Russia.

NOW YOU CAN Introduce people

▶1:34 **CONVERSATION MODEL** Read and listen.

A: Tom, this is Paula. Paula's my classmate.
B: Hi, Paula.
C: Hi, Tom. Nice to meet you.
B: Nice to meet you, too.

▶1:35 **RHYTHM AND INTONATION** Listen again and repeat. Then practice the Conversation Model with two other students.

CONVERSATION ACTIVATOR Personalize the conversation with two other students. Use your own names. Then change roles.

A: .... , this is .... 's my ....
B: Hi, ...
C: Hi, ... Nice to meet you.
B: Nice to meet you, too.

DON'T STOP!
Ask questions.

RECYCLE THIS LANGUAGE.
Where are you from?
What do you do?

CHANGE PARTNERS Introduce other classmates.

GOAL Tell someone your first and last name

1 ▶1:36 VOCABULARY • *Titles and names* Read and listen. Then listen again and repeat.

Titles	🧍	🧍	👰	🤵
1 Mr.	✓		✓	
2 Mrs.				✓ ✓✓
3 Miss		✓		
4 Ms.		✓		✓

Mr. Brendan Hu   Mrs. Lisa Hu
5 first name   **6** last name

Be careful!
Mr. Brendan Hu   OR   Mr. Hu
Mrs. Lisa Hu   OR   Mrs. Hu
NOT ~~Mr. Brendan~~
NOT ~~Mrs. Lisa~~

VOCABULARY BOOSTER
More titles • p. 126

2 **PAIR WORK** Introduce yourself to a classmate. Use a title and your last name.

❝ Hi. I'm Mr. Wilson. ❞

❝ Nice to meet you, Mr. Wilson. ❞

3 ▶1:37 LISTENING COMPREHENSION Listen. Circle the correct information. Then listen again and check your answers.

1
- ◉ Mr.
- ○ Mrs. (Craig) Bryant
- ○ Miss first name last name
- ○ Ms.

2
- ○ Mr.
- ○ Mrs. Brenda Corsun
- ○ Miss first name last name
- ◉ Ms.

3
- ◉ Mr.
- ○ Mrs. Damian Bao
- ○ Miss first name last name
- ○ Ms.

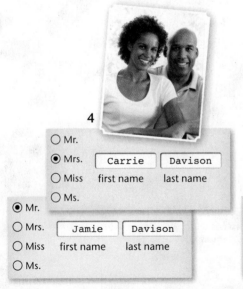

4
- ○ Mr.
- ◉ Mrs. Carrie Davison
- ○ Miss first name last name
- ○ Ms.

- ◉ Mr.
- ○ Mrs. Jamie Davison
- ○ Miss first name last name
- ○ Ms.

5
- ○ Mr.
- ○ Mrs Teresa Walder
- ◉ Miss first name last name
- ○ Ms.

6
- ○ Mr.
- ○ Mrs. Rita Bernal
- ○ Miss first name last name
- ◉ Ms.

- ◉ Mr.
- ○ Mrs. Mauricio Escobar
- ○ Miss first name last name
- ○ Ms.

You:

☒Mr.   ☐Mrs.   ☐Miss   ☐Ms.

Muherrem   _BAYAM_
first name   last name

A classmate:

☒ Mr.   _Adem_
☐ Mrs.   first name
☐ Miss   _ÖNAL_
☐ Ms.   last name

Your teacher:

☒ Mr.   ☐ Mrs.   ☐ Miss   ☐ Ms.

Joir   _Gomez_
first name   last name

NOW YOU CAN   Tell someone your first and last name

▶1:38 CONVERSATION MODEL   Read and listen.

A: What's your last name, please?
B: Fava.
A: And your first name?
B: My first name? Bob.

A: Thank you, Mr. Fava.
B: You're welcome.

▶1:39 RHYTHM AND INTONATION   Listen again and repeat.
Then practice the Conversation Model with a partner.

CONVERSATION ACTIVATOR   With a partner, personalize the
conversation. Use your own names. Write your partner's
information on the form. Then change roles.

A: What's your last name, please?
B: ....
A: And your first name?
B: My first name? ....
A: Thank you, ...
B: You're welcome.

☐ Mr.
☐ Mrs. _____ _____
☐ Miss   first name   last name
☐ Ms.

DON'T STOP!
Ask more questions.

RECYCLE THIS LANGUAGE.
How do you spell that?
What do you do?
Where are you from?

CHANGE PARTNERS   Personalize the conversation again.

GOAL Get someone's contact information

1 ▶1:40 **VOCABULARY • *Numbers 0–20*** Read and listen. Then listen again and repeat.

DIGITAL FLASH CARDS

0 zero **7** seven **14** fourteen

1 one **8** eight **15** fifteen

2 two **9** nine **16** sixteen

3 three **10** ten **17** seventeen

4 four **11** eleven **18** eighteen

5 five **12** twelve **19** nineteen

6 six **13** thirteen **20** twenty

2 **PAIR WORK** Read a number aloud from the picture. Your partner writes the number on a separate piece of paper.

3 **GRAMMAR • *Be: information questions with What***

What's his name?	(Mark Crandall.)
What's his last name?	(Crandall.)
What's Ellen's address?	(18 Main Street.)
What's her e-mail address?	(Dover14@hipnet.com.)
What's her occupation?	(She's a writer.)
What's their phone number?	(835-555-0037.)
What are their first names?	(Luis and Samuel.)

What is ➔ **What's**

How to say e-mail addresses and phone numbers:
Say "dover fourteen **at** hipnet **dot** com."
Say *"oh"* for *zero*: 0037 = *"oh-oh-three-seven."*

4 ▶1:41 **PRONUNCIATION • *Stress in two-word pairs*** Read and listen. Then listen again and repeat.

DIGITAL VIDEO COACH

● ·
first name

● · ·
phone num ber

● · · ·
e-mail address

5 ▶1:42 **LISTENING COMPREHENSION** Listen to the conversations. Write the information. Then listen again and check your work.

NAME		PHONE NUMBER	E-MAIL	
Valerie	Peterson	0522 295.12	mb	@
Mathilda	EIYAKIN	__-555-4500		
Jemies	Quinn	__-____	____ ' @ .com
Joseph	park	110-__-__-67	

1 A: *What's his* address?
B: 11 Main Street.

2 A: *What's her* phone number?
B: 22-63-140.

3 A: *What's their* address?
B: 18 Bank Street.

4 A: *What's his* phone number?
B: 878-456-0055.

5 A: *What's her* e-mail address?
B: It's sgast@mp.net.

6 A: *What's their* phone number?
B: 44-78-35.

NOW YOU CAN Get someone's contact information

▶1:43 **CONVERSATION MODEL** Read and listen.

A: What's your name?
B: Dave Mitchell.
A: And what's your phone number?
B: 523-6620.
A: 523-6620?
B: That's right. —Doğru

▶1:44 **RHYTHM AND INTONATION** Listen again and repeat.
Then practice the Conversation Model with a partner.

CONVERSATION ACTIVATOR With a partner, personalize the conversation. Write your partner's answers on a separate sheet of paper. Then change roles.

A: What's your .... ?
B: ....
A: And what's your .... ?
B: ....
A: .... ?
B: That's right.

DON'T STOP!

Continue the conversation.
Ask more questions.

RECYCLE THIS LANGUAGE.

first name / last name
address / e-mail address
Thank you.
You're welcome.
Nice to meet you.
Good-bye.

CHANGE PARTNERS Get other classmates' contact information.

EXTENSION

1 ▶1:45 **READING** Read about six famous people. Where are they from?

This is Nadia Santini. Where is Ms. Santini from? She's from Italy. And what's her occupation? She's a chef.

This is Chris Botti, from the U.S. What's his occupation? He's a musician.

This is Li Na. She's from China. What's Ms. Li's occupation? She's an athlete.

This is Vincent Lam. Mr. Lam has two occupations. He's a doctor and a writer. He's from Canada.

This is Diana Haddad. What's her occupation? Ms. Haddad is a singer. She's from Lebanon.

This is Sophie Okoneda. Ms. Okoneda is from the U.K. What's her occupation? She's an actor.

DIGITAL
MORE
EXERCISES

2 **PAIR WORK** Ask and answer questions about people in the Reading. Use the verb <u>be</u>.

❝ Is Nadia Santini a doctor? ❞   ❝ Is Vincent Lam from the United States? ❞   ❝ Where's Ms. Okoneda from? ❞

3 **SPEAKING** Point to the people in the photos. Ask your partner questions about their contact information.

Peter Matson
🏠 22 Bank St.
ⓔ pmatson@ccc.com

Lisa Kim
☎ 25-61-0078
ⓔ lisa.kim@hipnet.com

Fran Green   Bill Green
☎ 34-67-9899
🏠 13 Quinn St.

GRAMMAR BOOSTER
Unit 2 review • p. 136

For additional language practice . . .

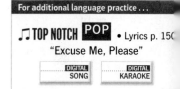

♫ TOP NOTCH **POP** • Lyrics p. 150
"Excuse Me, Please"

DIGITAL SONG   DIGITAL KARAOKE

PERSONAL INFORMATION

First name:	Last name:
Address:	
Phone:	e-mail:

PAIR WORK

1 Create a conversation for the people in Photo 1. Complete the form with your partner's information. Start like this:

What's your ___?

2 Create a conversation for the people in Photo 2. Introduce the man and the woman. Start like this:

This is ___. He's my ___.

WRITING Write sentences about your relationships. For example:

Nancy is my friend. She's a student. Her last name is Lee. She's from Vancouver. Ryan is my colleague. He's a . . .

WRITING BOOSTER p. 146
Guidance for this writing exercise

✓ NOW I CAN

☐ Introduce people.
☐ Tell someone my first and last name.
☐ Get someone's contact information.

COMMUNICATION GOALS
1 Talk about locations.
2 Discuss how to get places.
3 Discuss transportation.

UNIT 3 Places and How to Get There

LESSON 1

GOAL Talk about locations

1 ▶1:48 VOCABULARY • *Places in the neighborhood* Read and listen. Then listen again and repeat.

1 a bank

2 a restaurant

3 a pharmacy

4 a school

5 a newsstand

6 a bookstore

VOCABULARY BOOSTER
More places • p. 126

2 ▶1:49 LISTENING COMPREHENSION Listen. Write the places you hear.

1 ...a bank...............   3 ...a farmcy...
2 ...a School...........   4 ...a bookstore...

3 PAIR WORK Say the name of a place. Your partner writes the word.

4 ▶1:50 VOCABULARY • *Locations* Read and listen. Then listen again and repeat.

1 across the street

2 down the street

3 around the corner

4 on the left

5 on the right

6 next to the bank

7 between the bookstore and the bank

PAIR WORK Take turns making statements about the places.

> The bank is across the street.

  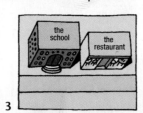  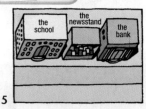

GRAMMAR • *Be: Questions with Where / Subject pronoun it*

Ask questions with Where for locations.
Where's the restaurant?

Contractions
Where is → Where's
It is → It's

Use it to replace the names of places.
It's down the street. (It = the restaurant)

▶1:51 **PRONUNCIATION** • *Falling intonation for questions with Where* Read and listen. Then listen again and repeat.

1 Where is it?

2 Where's the bank?

3 Where's the school?

4 Where's the newsstand?

7 **GRAMMAR PRACTICE** Read the sentences. Write questions and answers. Answer with It's.

1 The pharmacy is across the street.
   A: ...*Where's the pharmacy*............ ?
   B: ...*It's across the street*........... .

2 Billy's Restaurant is around the corner.
   A: .... ?
   B: ....

3 The newsstand is on the left.
   A: .... ?
   B: ....

4 The bookstore is next to the school.
   A: .... ?
   B: ....

NOW YOU CAN Talk about locations

▶1:52 **CONVERSATION MODEL**
Read and listen.

A: Excuse me. Where's the bank?
B: The bank? It's around the corner.
A: Thanks!
B: You're welcome.

▶1:53 **RHYTHM AND INTONATION**
Listen again and repeat. Then practice the Conversation Model with a partner.

CONVERSATION ACTIVATOR
With a partner, change the conversation. Find the people on the map. Talk about the location of the places. Then change roles.

A: Excuse me. Where's the .... ?
B: .... ? It's ....
A: Thanks!
B: You're welcome.

DON'T STOP!
Ask about another location.

CHANGE PARTNERS Ask about other locations.

1 ▶ 1:54 VOCABULARY • *Ways to get places* Read and listen. Then listen again and repeat.

1 walk   **2** drive   **3** take a taxi   **4** take the train   **5** take the bus

2 GRAMMAR • *The imperative*

Use imperatives to give instructions and directions.

Affirmative imperatives	Negative imperatives
Drive [to the bank].	Don't walk.
Take the bus [to the pharmacy].	Don't take the train.

Don't = Do not

Walk.
Don't drive.

3 VOCABULARY / GRAMMAR PRACTICE Follow the directions.

Partner A: Read a direction.
Partner B: Say the letter of the correct picture.

1 Walk to the bookstore.
2 Don't drive to the restaurant.
3 Take the bus to the bank.
4 Don't walk to the pharmacy.
5 Drive down the street.

Partner B: Read a direction.
Partner A: Say the letter of the correct picture.

6 Take the bus down the street.
7 Don't take the bus to the bank.
8 Walk to the bank.
9 Take a taxi to the restaurant.
10 Drive to the pharmacy.

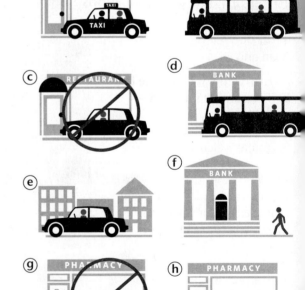

4 ▶1:55 LISTENING COMPREHENSION Listen. Write the directions. Use an affirmative and a negative imperative.

1 *Take the bus. Don't drive.* Restaurant 3 *Take the bus* 5 ....

2 *Drive. Don't walk* 4 .... *taxi*

1 ▶1:56 CONVERSATION MODEL Read and listen.

A: Can I walk to the bookstore?
B: The bookstore? Sure.
A: And what about the school?
B: The school? Don't walk. Drive.
A: OK. Thanks!

2 ▶1:57 RHYTHM AND INTONATION Listen again and repeat.
Then practice the Conversation Model with a partner.

3 CONVERSATION ACTIVATOR With a partner, change the
conversation, using the photos. Ask how to get to places
in the neighborhood. Then change roles.

A: Can I walk to the .... ?
B: The .... ? Sure.
A: And what about the .... ?
B: The .... ? Don't walk. ....
A: OK. Thanks!

DON'T STOP!
Talk about locations.

RECYCLE THIS LANGUAGE.
Where is it?

	across the street.
	down the street.
It's	around the corner.
	next to the ___.
	between the ___ and the ___.

CHANGE PARTNERS Ask about more places.

GOAL Discuss transportation

1 ▶1:58 **VOCABULARY** • *Means of transportation*   Read and listen. Then listen again and repeat.

1 a car

2 a bicycle

3 a moped

4 a subway

5 a motorcycle

Also remember:
a bus
a train
a taxi

2 **PAIR WORK** Take turns. Spell a vocabulary word aloud. Your partner writes the word.

3 **GRAMMAR** • **By** to express means

by taxi   by bicycle   by motorcycle

4 ▶1:59 **LISTENING COMPREHENSION** Listen. Circle the means of transportation you hear.

1

2

3

4

5

5 ▶1:60 **VOCABULARY • *Destinations*** Read and listen. Then listen again and repeat.

1 go to work

2 go home

3 go to school

6 ▶1:61 **LISTENING COMPREHENSION** Listen. Use a <u>by</u> phrase to write the means of transportation. Then check the box for work, home, or school.

Means of transportation			
1	by car		✓	
2	Solsbey.			
3	S cool.			
4	r			
5	boors.			
6	By taxi			

NOW YOU CAN **Discuss transportation**

▶1:62 **CONVERSATION MODEL**
Read and listen.

A: How do you go to school?
B: By subway. What about you?
A: Me? I walk.

▶1:63 **RHYTHM AND INTONATION**
Listen again and repeat. Then practice the Conversation Model with a partner.

CONVERSATION ACTIVATOR
With a partner, personalize the conversation. Ask about work, school, and home. Then change roles.

A: How do you go ....?
B: .... What about you?
A: Me? ....

CHANGE PARTNERS Personalize the conversation again.

EXTENSION

1 ▶ 1:64 **READING** Read about how people go to work and school.

1 I'm Mark Jackson. I'm an architect. My office is down the street from my home. I can walk to work. I'm lucky!

2 I'm a manager of a bank. My name is Laura Blake. I go to work by car with my neighbor from across the street, Brad Lane. We're colleagues at the bank.

3 I'm Min Park, and I'm a doctor from Miami. I go to work by train. I take the train home, too.

4 I'm Matt Carson, and this is my teacher, Mr. Green. My school is right around the corner from my home, so I walk to school with my friends. We walk home together, too.

5 I'm Art Green. I'm Matt's teacher. Can I walk to school? No way! My home is not around the corner from the school. I take the bus to and from school.

2 **PAIR WORK** Ask and answer the questions.

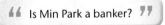

1 Is Mark Jackson a doctor?

2 Is Brad Lane Laura Blake's friend or her colleague?

3 Is Mr. Lane Ms. Blake's neighbor?

4 Is Matt Carson a student?

5 What is Matt's teacher's name?

6 Is Dr. Park from Miami?

7 Where is Mark Jackson's office?

8 Your own question: .... ?

66 Is Min Park a banker? 99

66 No, she's not. She's a doctor. 99

DIGITAL
**MORE
EXERCISES**

3 **GROUP WORK** On the board, make a map of places near your school. Write the names of the places. Then take turns describing the locations of the places.

RECYCLE THIS LANGUAGE.

Where's the [pharmacy]?	Walk. Don't [drive].
It's ___.	Go by [bus].
Can I [walk] to the [restaurant]?	Don't go by [train].
Take / Don't take the [bus].	

GRAMMAR BOOSTER
Unit 3 review • p. 137

REVIEW

CONTEST Study the picture for one minute. Then close your books. Who can remember all of the locations? For example:

The school is down the street.

PAIR WORK Create conversations for the people. For example:

A: *How do you go to work?*
B: *By bus.*

WRITING Write five questions and answers about locations in the picture for the people at the bus stop. For example:

Where's the restaurant?
It's across the street.

WRITING BOOSTER p. 146
Guidance for this writing exercise

SCHOOL

PHARMACY

RESTAURANT

RESTAURANT   BANK

BOOKS

NEWS

BUS

SUBWAY

✔ NOW I CAN

☐ Talk about locations.
☐ Discuss how to get places.
☐ Discuss transportation.

COMMUNICATION GOALS
1   Identify people in your family.
2   Describe your relatives.
3   Talk about your family.

UNIT 4 Family

LESSON 1 **GOAL** Identify people in your family

1 ▶ 2:02 **VOCABULARY** • *Family relationships*   Read and listen. Then listen again and repeat.

1 grandparents →

2 grandmother   **3** grandfather

10 grandchildren
11 grandson   **12** granddaughter

4 parents →

5 mother   **6** father

13 wife   **14** husband

7 children*
* one **child** / two **children**

8 daughter   **9** son

15 sister   **16** brother

2 **PAIR WORK** Point to two people in the family. Describe their relationship.   *" She's his daughter. "*

3 ▶ 2:03 **LISTENING COMPREHENSION** Listen to a man identify people in his family. Check the correct photo.

1

☐   ☐

2

☐   ☐

3

☐   ☐

4

☐   ☐

5
 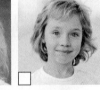
☐   ☐

6

☐   ☐

4 GRAMMAR • _Be_: questions with _Who_

Who **is** he? (He's my dad.*)	Who **are** they? (They're my sisters.)
Who**'s** Louise? (She's my mom.*)	Who **are** Nina and Jan? (They're my daughters.)

Contractions
Who is → **Who's**

Be careful!
Who are NOT ~~Who're~~

* <u>mom</u> and <u>dad</u> = informal for <u>mother</u> and <u>father</u>

5 GRAMMAR PRACTICE Write questions. Use <u>Who's</u> or <u>Who are</u> and <u>he</u>, <u>she</u>, or <u>they</u>.

1 **A:** .....Who's he............... ?
  B: He's my grandfather.

2 **A:** .... ?
  B: She's my mother.

3 **A:** .... ?
  B: He's Mr. Fine's grandson.

4 **A:** .... ?
  B: They're Pat's grandparents.

5 **A:** .... ?
  B: She's Ed's wife.

6 **A:** .... ?
  B: They're my brother and sister.

NOW YOU CAN Identify people in your family

▶ 2:04 **CONVERSATION MODEL** Read and listen.

A: Who's that?
B: That's my father.
A: And who are they?
B: They're my sisters, Mindy and Jen.

▶ 2:05 **RHYTHM AND INTONATION** Listen again and repeat. Then practice the Conversation Model with a partner.

CONVERSATION ACTIVATOR Bring in photos of the people in your family (OR write their names). With a partner, personalize the conversation. Then change roles.

A: Who's that?
B: That's ....
A: And .... ?
B: ....

DON'T STOP!
Talk about occupations.
Ask more questions.

RECYCLE THIS LANGUAGE.
He's / She's [an engineer].
They're [architects].
What's his / her name?
What are their names?
How do you spell that?

CHANGE PARTNERS Personalize the conversation again.

GOAL Describe your relatives

1 ▶2:06 VOCABULARY • *Adjectives to describe people*
Read and listen. Then listen again and repeat.

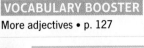
VOCABULARY BOOSTER
More adjectives • p. 127

5 pretty   **6** handsome

1 short   **2** tall   **3** old   **4** young

7 good-looking

8 cute

2 GRAMMAR • *Be* with adjectives / Adverbs *very* and *so*

Describe people with a form of *be* and an adjective.
She's pretty.   They're good-looking.
He's handsome.   Your children are cute.

The adverbs *very* and *so* make adjectives stronger.
They're very good-looking.   She's so pretty.
He's very handsome.   Your children are so cute.

very = !
so = !!!

3 PAIR WORK Use the Vocabulary to describe people in your class.

" Gina and Deborah are very pretty. "

4 ▶2:07 LISTENING COMPREHENSION Listen to the conversations.
Circle the adjective that describes each person.

1 Her husband is (handsome / tall / old).

2 His daughter is (tall / good-looking / cute).

3 Her brothers are (tall / good-looking / young).

4 His son is (tall / good-looking / short).

5 Her father is (tall / old / short).

6 His sisters are (tall / good-looking / short).

5 VOCABULARY / GRAMMAR PRACTICE Look at the photos. Complete each
sentence with a form of *be* and an adjective.

1 Your sisters ....
so ....

2 Your daughter ....
so ....!

3 Our grandfather ....
very ....

4 Her boyfriend .... very ....

5 His wife .... so .... !

6 Her brother .... very ....

VOCABULARY / GRAMMAR PRACTICE Write three sentences about people in your family. Use adjectives and the adverbs <u>very</u> or <u>so</u> to describe the people.

1 ....

2 ....

3 ....

> My mother is very tall.

NOW YOU CAN Describe your relatives

▶2:08 **CONVERSATION MODEL** Read and listen.

A: Tell me about your father.
B: Well, he's a doctor. And he's very tall.
A: And how about your mother?
B: She's an engineer. She's very pretty.

▶2:09 **RHYTHM AND INTONATION** Listen again and repeat. Then practice the Conversation Model with a partner.

CONVERSATION ACTIVATOR With a partner, personalize the conversation. Describe your relatives. Then change roles.

A: Tell me about your ....
B: Well, ... And ....
A: And how about your .... ?
B: ....

DON'T STOP!
Ask about other people in your partner's family.

CHANGE PARTNERS Ask about other classmates' relatives.

GOAL Talk about your family

1 **GRAMMAR • Verb _have_ / _has_: affirmative statements**

> I have one son and one daughter.

| I
You
We
They | have a brother. | He
She | has three sisters. |

2 **GRAMMAR PRACTICE** Complete the sentences. Use <u>have</u> or <u>has</u>. Then complete the sentence about your own family.

1 Mark .... two brothers.

2 Mrs. Stevens .... five grandsons.

3 They .... a granddaughter.

4 We .... twelve grandchildren.

5 Carl and Anna .... two children.

6 She .... five sisters.

7 They .... no brothers or sisters.

YOU I ....

DIGITAL MORE EXERCISES

3 ▶ 2:10 **VOCABULARY • _Numbers 21–101_** Read and listen. Then listen again and repeat.

DIGITAL FLASH CARDS

21 twenty-one	**25** twenty-five	**29** twenty-nine	**40** forty	**80** eighty
22 twenty-two	**26** twenty-six	**30** thirty	**50** fifty	**90** ninety
23 twenty-three	**27** twenty-seven	**31** thirty-one	**60** sixty	**100** one hundred
24 twenty-four	**28** twenty-eight	**32** thirty-two	**70** seventy	**101** one hundred one

DIGITAL VIDEO COACH

4 ▶ 2:11 **PRONUNCIATION • _Numbers_** Listen and repeat. Then practice saying the numbers on your own.

13 · 30	17 · 70
14 · 40	18 · 80
15 · 50	19 · 90
16 · 60	

5 **PAIR WORK** Take turns saying a number from the chart. Your partner circles the number.

23	45	40	18	94	21	20	14
58	102	43	89	90	44	53	13
30	19	60	99	22	50	52	100
15	47	33	54	17	66	77	70
64	78	95	80	87	101	1	31

GRAMMAR • *Be: questions with How old*

How old is	he?	(He's nineteen years old.)
	she?	(She's thirty-three.)
	your sister?	(She's twenty.)
How old are	they?	(They're twenty-nine.)
	your parents?	(They're fifty and fifty-two.)

7 GRAMMAR PRACTICE Complete the questions. Use How old is or How old are.

1 .... your sister?

2 .... Matt's parents?

3 .... your grandfather?

4 .... Helen's husband?

5 .... her children?

6 .... his son?

NOW YOU CAN Talk about your family

1 ▶2:12 CONVERSATION MODEL Read and listen.

A: I have one brother and two sisters.
B: Really? How old is your brother?
A: Twenty.
B: And your sisters?
A: Eighteen and twenty-two.

2 ▶2:13 RHYTHM AND INTONATION Listen again and repeat. Then practice the Conversation Model with a partner.

CONVERSATION ACTIVATOR With a partner, personalize the conversation. Talk about your own family. Then change roles.

A: I have ....
B: Really? How old .... ?
A: ....
B: And your .... ?
A: ....

DON'T STOP!
Ask more questions.

RECYCLE THIS LANGUAGE.

Tell me about your [mother].
And your [father]?
How about your [grandparents]?

What's his / her name?
What are their names?

What's his / her occupation?
What are their occupations?

CHANGE PARTNERS Personalize the conversation again.

EXTENSION

1   ▶ 2:14 **READING** Read about some famous actors and their families and friends.

Who Are They?

This is **Gael García Bernal**, on the left, with his good friend, **Diego Luna**, on the right. Mr. García Bernal is a famous actor from Mexico. His parents, Patricia Bernal and José Ángel García, are actors, too. He has one sister and two brothers. Mr. Luna is also an actor. Many people think they are both very handsome.

Dakota Fanning is a movie actor. Her younger sister, **Elle**, is also an actor in movies. They are from the United States, and they are both very pretty. Their father, Steven Fanning, is a salesman, and their mother, Heather Joy, is an athlete. Dakota and Elle are also students.

Meet **Jay Chou**, a famous singer from Taiwan. He is also an excellent musician and an actor. His parents are both teachers. Mr. Chou has no brothers or sisters. His girlfriend is **Hannah Quinlivan**. Her father is from Australia, and her mother is from Taiwan. Her Chinese name is Kun Ling. She is very young and pretty.

2   **READING COMPREHENSION** Read about the people again. Complete the sentences.

1 Gael García Bernal is Diego Luna's ....

2 Patricia Bernal, José Ángel García, and Diego Luna are all ....

3 Heather Joy is Steven Fanning's ....

4 Elle Fanning is Heather Joy's ....

5 Mr. Chou's .... is good-looking.

6 Jay Chou's parents have one ....

3   **PAIR WORK** Interview your partner. Complete the notepad with information about your partner's family.

Relative's name	Relationship	Age	Occupation	Description
Doug	brother	14	student	He's very tall.

Relative's name	Relationship	Age	Occupation	Description

GRAMMAR BOOSTER
Unit 4 review • p. 137

For additional language practice . . .

4   **GROUP WORK** Now tell your classmates about your partner's family.

"" Doug is Laura's brother. He's 14. . . . ""

♫ **TOP NOTCH** **POP** • Lyrics p. 15
"Tell Me All About It"

DIGITAL SONG   DIGITAL KARAOKE

PAIR WORK

1 Ask and answer questions about the people in the two photos. For example:

A: *Who's Ellen?*
B: *She's Natalie's mother.*
A: *Is Mia Ellen's daughter?*
B: *No, she's not. She's her . . .*

2 Take turns making statements about the family relationships. For example:

Matt has two children. Nora is his daughter.

DESCRIPTION Choose a photo. Use adjectives to describe the people in each family. For example:

Mia is very cute.

WRITING Choose two of your relatives. Write sentences about them. For example:

> *My sister is 24 years old. She's short and good-looking. She's an architect. Her name is . . .*

WRITING BOOSTER p.147
Guidance for this writing exercise

✔ NOW I CAN

- ☐ Identify people in my family.
- ☐ Describe my relatives.
- ☐ Talk about my family.

COMMUNICATION GOALS

1 Confirm that you're on time.
2 Talk about the time of an event.
3 Ask about birthdays.

Events and Times

LESSON 1 **GOAL** Confirm that you're on time

 1 ▶2:17 VOCABULARY • *What time is it?* Read and listen. Then listen again and repeat.

1 It's one o'clock.

2 It's one fifteen. OR
It's a quarter after one.

3 It's one twenty. OR
It's twenty after one.

4 It's one thirty. OR
It's half past one.

0:00 to 11:59 = A.M.
12:00 to 23:59 = P.M.

Say "eight A.M."
or "eight P.M."

5 It's one forty. OR
It's twenty to two.

6 It's one forty-five. OR
It's a quarter to two.

7 It's noon.

8 It's midnight.

2 ▶2:18 PRONUNCIATION • *Sentence rhythm* Read and listen.
Then listen again and repeat.

1 It's TEN after FIVE.   2 It's TWENty to ONE.   3 It's a QUARter to TWO.

3 PRONUNCIATION PRACTICE Read the times in the Vocabulary aloud again.
Pay attention to sentence rhythm.

4 PAIR WORK Look at the
map. Ask your partner
about times around the
world. Say each time
two ways.

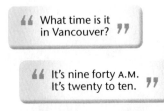

❝ What time is it
in Vancouver? ❞

❝ It's nine forty A.M.
It's twenty to ten. ❞

36   UNIT 5

5 ▶ 2:19 **VOCABULARY** • *Early, on time, and late* Read and listen. Then listen again and repeat.

1 She's **early**.

2 They're **on time**.

3 He's **late**.

NOW YOU CAN Confirm that you're on time

1 ▶ 2:20 **CONVERSATION MODEL** Read and listen.

A: What time is the meeting?
B: 10:00.
A: Uh-oh. Am I late?
B: No, you're not. It's five to ten.
A: Five to ten?
B: That's right. You're early.

2 ▶ 2:21 **RHYTHM AND INTONATION** Listen again and repeat. Then practice the Conversation Model with a partner.

3 **CONVERSATION ACTIVATOR** With a partner, change the conversation. Use the pictures and the times. Then change roles.

A: What time is the .... ?
B: ....
A: Uh-oh. Am I late?
B: .... It's ....
A: .... ?
B: That's right. You're ....

Class: 2:15 P.M.
Time now: 2:15 P.M.

Train: 2:30 P.M.
Time now: 2:35 P.M.

Bus: 2:00 P.M.
Time now: 1:50 P.M.

CHANGE PARTNERS Change the conversation again.

VOCABULARY BOOSTER
More events • p. 127

1 ▶2:22 VOCABULARY • *Events* Read and listen. Then listen again and repeat.

1 a party

2 a dance

3 a game

4 a dinner

5 a movie

6 a concert

2 ▶2:23 LISTENING COMPREHENSION Listen to the conversations about events.
Write the event and circle the time.

1 .... (7:15 / 7:45) 4 .... (12:00 A.M. / 12:00 P.M.)
2 .... (8:00 / 9:00) 5 .... (9:15 / 9:50)
3 .... (3:30 / 3:15) 6 .... (12:00 A.M. / 12:00 P.M.)

3 ▶2:24 VOCABULARY • *Days of the week* Read and listen. Then listen again and repeat.

WEEKDAYS					THE WEEKEND	
Monday	Tuesday	Wednesday	Thursday	Friday	Saturday	Sunday

4 GRAMMAR • <u>Be</u>: *questions about time / Prepositions* <u>at</u> *and* <u>on</u>

What time is it? (It's) five twenty.
What time's the party? (It's) at nine thirty.
What day is the concert? (It's) on Saturday.

When's the dance? (It's) at ten o'clock.
(It's) on Friday at 10:00 P.M.

Contractions
What time is → **What time's**
What day is → **What day's**
When is → **When's**

Be careful!
What time is it? NOT What ~~time's~~ it?
When is it? NOT ~~When's~~ it?

5 GRAMMAR PRACTICE Complete the questions and answers. Use contractions when possible.

1 A: When .... the party?
B: It's .... 11:00 P.M.

2 A: .... day's the game?
B: It's .... Saturday.

3 A: What .... the concert?
B: It's .... 8:30.

4 A: What .... the dinner?
B: It's .... Tuesday.

5 A: .... the dance?
B: It's .... Friday at 9:00.

6 A: What .... the class?
B: It's .... noon.

6 ▶2:25 LISTENING COMPREHENSION Listen to the conversation. Write the events on the calendar.

	Monday		Thursday	
	5:30		5:30	
	6:30		6:30	
	7:00		7:00	*meeting*
	7:15		7:15	

Tuesday		Friday	
5:30		5:30	
6:30		6:30	
7:00		7:00	
7:15		7:15	

Wednesday		Saturday		Sunday	
5:30		5:30		5:30	
6:30		6:30		6:30	
7:00		7:00		7:00	
7:15		7:15		7:15	

NOW YOU CAN Talk about the time of an event

▶2:26 CONVERSATION MODEL Read and listen.

A: Look. There's a dance on Wednesday.
B: Great! What time?
A: 10:30. At Pat's Restaurant.
B: Really? Let's meet at 10:15.

▶2:27 RHYTHM AND INTONATION Listen again and repeat. Then practice the Conversation Model with a partner.

CONVERSATION ACTIVATOR With a partner, change the conversation. Ask about an event. Use these events or your own events. Then change roles.

A: Look. There's a .... on ....
B: Great! What time?
A: .... At ....
B: Really? Let's meet at ....

School Dance
WEDNESDAY, 10:30 P.M.
Pat's Restaurant

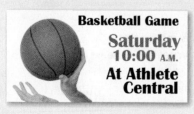

Basketball Game
Saturday
10:00 A.M.
At Athlete Central

MOVIE NIGHT
Space Pilot
Thursday, **9:00** P.M.
Mercy's Books

School Dinner
Saturday, 8:00 P.M.
Hank's Restaurant

Concert
FRIDAY, 8:00
AT PARKER HALL

CHANGE PARTNERS Talk about different events.

DIGITAL FLASH CARDS

1 ▶2:28 VOCABULARY • *Ordinal numbers* Read and listen. Then listen again and repeat.

1st first	**2nd** second	**3rd** third	**4th** fourth	**5th** fifth
6th sixth	**7th** seventh	**8th** eighth	**9th** ninth	**10th** tenth
11th eleventh	**12th** twelfth	**13th** thirteenth	**14th** fourteenth	**15th** fifteenth
16th sixteenth	**17th** seventeenth	**18th** eighteenth	**19th** nineteenth	**20th** twentieth
21st twenty-first	**22nd** twenty-second	**30th** thirtieth	**40th** fortieth	**50th** fiftieth

2 PAIR WORK Say a number. Your partner says the ordinal number.

" three "   " third "

3 ▶2:29 VOCABULARY • *Months of the year* Read and listen.
Then listen again and repeat.

January
S	M	T	W	T	F	S
			1	2	3	4
5	6	7	8	9	10	11
12	13	14	15	16	17	18
19	20	21	22	23	24	25
26	27	28	29	30	31	

February
S	M	T	W	T	F	S
						1
2	3	4	5	6	7	8
9	10	11	12	13	14	15
16	17	18	19	20	21	22
23	24	25	26	27	28	

March
S	M	T	W	T	F	S
						1
2	3	4	5	6	7	8
9	10	11	12	13	14	15
16	17	18	19	20	21	22
23	24	25	26	27	28	29
30	31					

April
S	M	T	W	T	F	S
		1	2	3	4	5
6	7	8	9	10	11	12
13	14	15	16	17	18	19
20	21	22	23	24	25	26
27	28	29	30			

May
S	M	T	W	T	F	S
				1	2	3
4	5	6	7	8	9	10
11	12	13	14	15	16	17
18	19	20	21	22	23	24
25	26	27	28	29	30	31

June
S	M	T	W	T	F	S
1	2	3	4	5	6	
8	9	10	11	12	13	
15	16	17	18	19	20	
22	23	24	25	26	27	
29	30					

July
S	M	T	W	T	F	S
		1	2	3	4	5
6	7	8	9	10	11	12
13	14	15	16	17	18	19
20	21	22	23	24	25	26
27	28	29	30	31		

August
S	M	T	W	T	F	S
					1	2
3	4	5	6	7	8	9
10	11	12	13	14	15	16
17	18	19	20	21	22	23
24	25	26	27	28	29	30
31						

September
S	M	T	W	T	F	S
	1	2	3	4	5	6
7	8	9	10	11	12	13
14	15	16	17	18	19	20
21	22	23	24	25	26	27
28	29	30				

October
S	M	T	W	T	F	S
			1	2	3	4
5	6	7	8	9	10	11
12	13	14	15	16	17	18
19	20	21	22	23	24	25
26	27	28	29	30	31	

November
S	M	T	W	T	F	S
						1
2	3	4	5	6	7	8
9	10	11	12	13	14	15
16	17	18	19	20	21	22
23	24	25	26	27	28	29
30						

December
S	M	T	W	T	F	
	1	2	3	4	5	
7	8	9	10	11	12	
14	15	16	17	18	19	
21	22	23	24	25	26	
28	29	30	31			

4 ▶2:30 LISTENING COMPREHENSION Listen to the dates. Circle the dates on the calendar.

5 PAIR WORK Say a date from the calendar. Your partner writes the date.

" July thirty-first "   July 31st

GRAMMAR • *Prepositions in, on, and at for dates and times: summary*

When's the party?	It's **in** January.	
When's the dance?	It's **on** January 15th.	
When's the dinner?	It's **on** the 12th.	
What day's the meeting?	It's **on** Tuesday.	
What time's the movie?	It's **at** noon.	
What time's the dance?	It's **at** 8:30.	

Be careful!
in the morning
in the afternoon
in the evening
BUT **at** night

The concert's **on** August 12th.

7 **GRAMMAR PRACTICE** Complete the sentences. Use <u>in</u>, <u>on</u>, or <u>at</u>.

1 The concert is .... July 14th .... 3:00 .... the afternoon.

2 The dinner is .... December .... the 6th.

3 The party is .... midnight .... Saturday.

4 The movie is .... November 1st .... 8:30 P.M.

5 The game is .... Wednesday .... noon.

6 The meeting is at the State Bank .... 11:00 .... the morning .... July 18th.

NOW YOU CAN | **Ask about birthdays**

▶2:31 **CONVERSATION MODEL** Read and listen.

A: When's your birthday?
B: On July 15th. When's <u>your</u> birthday?
A: My birthday's in November. On the 13th.

▶2:32 **RHYTHM AND INTONATION** Listen again and repeat. Then practice the Conversation Model with a partner.

CONVERSATION ACTIVATOR With a partner, personalize the conversation.

A: When's your birthday?
B: .... When's <u>your</u> birthday?
A: My birthday's ....

DON'T STOP!

Ask your partner questions about other people's birthdays. Complete the chart.

▶2:33 On someone's birthday say:

❝ Happy birthday! ❞

❝ Thank you! ❞

brother's birthday:	
sister's birthday:	
mother's birthday:	
father's birthday:	
grandmother's birthday:	
grandfather's birthday:	

CHANGE PARTNERS Ask about other people's birthdays.

EXTENSION

1 ▶2:34 **READING** Read the announcements. What are the events this week?

The Daily Express
Events for the week of June 20th

PARTY

June 21st is Sally Neufield's birthday!

90 years old, and so young!

When: Tuesday, June 21st, 7:00 P.M.

Where: Chuck's Café, around the corner from the bank. Don't be late!

MOVIE

English actor Peter Sellers in *The Party*

An oldie but goodie!

Friday, June 24th at 8:30 P.M.

At the New School 58 Post Street

DANCE

Both young and old are welcome!

Where: Casey's Restaurant, on Main Street, next to the Mrs. Books Bookstore

When: Saturday, June 25th at 8:30 P.M.

MEETING

Bank Managers Association

Thursday, June 23rd, from 9:00 A.M. to 2:00 P.M.

At Family Bank 58 New Street

Between Kim's Newsstand and Carson's Bookstore

GAME

Volleyball!

Sunday, June 26th 2:00 P.M.

Branfield School on Fitch Avenue, between 1st Street and 2nd Street

2 **READING COMPREHENSION** Correct all the mistakes. Use information from the Reading.

1 The dance is at half past ~~nine~~. *eight*

2 The movie is at 8:30 A.M.

3 The meeting is at 2:00 P.M.

4 The birthday party is at midnight.

5 The birthday party is on the 22nd.

6 The dance is at the bookstore.

7 The meeting is at the New School.

8 The party is at Casey's restaurant.

9 Branfield School is between a newsstand and a bookstore.

10 The game is on Saturday.

 DIGITAL MORE EXERCISES

3 **GROUP WORK** Ask about classmates' birthdays. Complete the chart.

Capricorn Dec. 22 – Jan. 20

Aquarius Jan. 21–Feb. 19

Pisces Feb. 20 – Mar. 20

Aries Mar. 21 – Apr. 20

Taurus Apr. 21– May 21

Sagittarius Nov. 22 – Dec. 21

Gemini May 22 – Jun. 21

Scorpio Oct. 23 – Nov. 21

Libra Sep. 23 – Oct. 22

Virgo Aug. 24 – Sep. 22

Leo Jul. 23 – Aug. 23

Cancer Jun. 22 – Jul. 22

Name	Birthday	Zodiac Sign

GRAMMAR BOOSTER
Unit 5 review • p. 138

For additional language practice...

♫ **TOP NOTCH** POP • Lyrics p. 15
"Let's Make a Date"

 DIGITAL SONG
 DIGITAL KARAOKE

PAIR WORK Create conversations for the people.

1 Talk about the events. For example:

Look. There's a ___ . . .

2 Confirm that you are on time for an event. For example:

What time's the ___?

CONTEST Study the events for one minute. Then close your books. Who can remember all the times, dates, and locations? For example:

There's a ___ on ___ at ___ .

WRITING Write five sentences about the events or ones in your town. For example:

There's a dinner on Friday, May 20th at . . .

WRITING BOOSTER p. 147
Guidance for this writing exercise

DINNER

When:
Friday, May 20th (8:30 P.M.)

Where:
My French Restaurant

Between the 13th Street School and the Corner Pharmacy

BASKETBALL GAME

Sunday, May 22, noon
At the Twelfth Night School

"Evening" in Concert!

When:
10:30 P.M., Tuesday, May 24
Where: Paul's Books (Next to UMS Bank)

MAY
20
FRIDAY

Party
Welcome all students!
Saturday, May 28
9:30 P.M.

Where? 58 Post Street
(across from the bank)

✓ **NOW I CAN**

☐ Confirm that I'm on time.
☐ Talk about the time of an event.
☐ Ask about birthdays.

UNIT **6** Clothes

COMMUNICATION GOALS
1 Give and accept a compliment.
2 Ask for colors and sizes.
3 Describe clothes.

LESSON **1** **GOAL** Give and accept a compliment

VOCABULARY BOOSTER
More clothes • p. 128

1 ▶2:37 VOCABULARY • *Clothes* Read and listen. Then listen again and repeat.

1 a shirt
2 a sweater
3 a tie
4 a jacket
5 a skirt
6 shoes
7 a dress
8 a suit
9 a blouse
10 pants*

* Pants is a plural noun. Use <u>are</u>, not <u>is</u>, with <u>pants</u>.

2 ▶2:38 PRONUNCIATION • *Plural nouns* Read and listen. Then listen again and repeat.

1 /s/	shirts = shirt/s/	2 /z/	shoes = shoe/z/	3 /ɪz/	blouses = blouse/ɪz/
	jackets = jacket/s/		sweaters = sweater/z/		dresses = dress/ɪz/

3 GRAMMAR • *Demonstratives* <u>this</u>, <u>that</u>, <u>these</u>, <u>those</u>

this sweater
that sweater
these ties
those ties

4 VOCABULARY / GRAMMAR PRACTICE Look at the pictures. Write <u>this</u>, <u>that</u>, <u>these</u>, or <u>those</u> and the name of the clothe

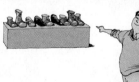

1 those jackets
2 ....
3 ....
4 ....

5 .... 6 .... 7 .... 8 ....

5 GRAMMAR • The simple present tense: affirmative statements with like, want, need, and have

Tina **likes** these shoes. She **wants** that shirt.

Rob **needs** a book. Now he **has** a book.

I You We They Sara and Jim	like want need have	those sweaters.
He She Cassie Ivan	likes wants needs has	those sweaters, too.

For **he**, **she**, and **it**, add **-s** to the base form.

like	→	**likes**
want	→	**wants**
need	→	**needs**
BUT: have	→	**has**

GRAMMAR PRACTICE Complete each statement with the correct form of the verb.

1 I .... your tie.
<u>like / likes</u>

2 My friends .... this suit.
<u>want / wants</u>

3 Janet .... this skirt.
<u>need / needs</u>

4 Peter .... that jacket.
<u>have / has</u>

5 We .... our dresses.
<u>like / likes</u>

6 Sue and Tara .... those suits.
<u>want / wants</u>

NOW YOU CAN Give and accept a compliment

▶2:39 **CONVERSATION MODEL** Read and listen.

A: I really like that dress.
B: Really?
A: Yes. And I like those shoes, too!
B: Thank you!
A: You're welcome.

▶2:40 **RHYTHM AND INTONATION** Listen again and repeat.
Then practice the Conversation Model with a partner.

CONVERSATION ACTIVATOR Personalize the conversation.
Compliment your partner on his or her clothes and
shoes. Then change roles.

A: I really like ....
B: Really?
A: Yes. And I like .... , too!
B: .... !
A: You're welcome.

DON'T STOP!
Talk about other clothes.

CHANGE PARTNERS Compliment other classmates' clothes.

1 ▶ 2:41 VOCABULARY • *Colors and sizes* Read and listen. Then listen again and repeat.

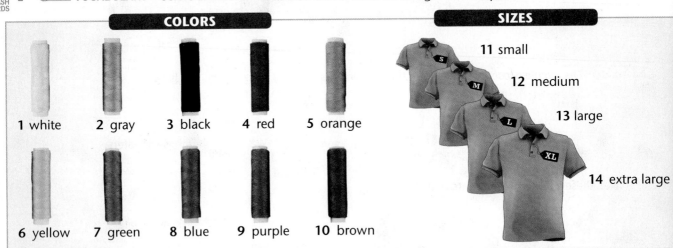

COLORS
1 white   2 gray   3 black   4 red   5 orange
6 yellow   7 green   8 blue   9 purple   10 brown

SIZES
11 small
12 medium
13 large
14 extra large

2 PAIR WORK Make two statements about your clothes.

My shoes are brown. My shirt is medium.

3 GRAMMAR • *The simple present tense: negative statements and <u>yes</u> / <u>no</u> questions with <u>like</u>, <u>want</u>, <u>need</u>, and <u>have</u>*

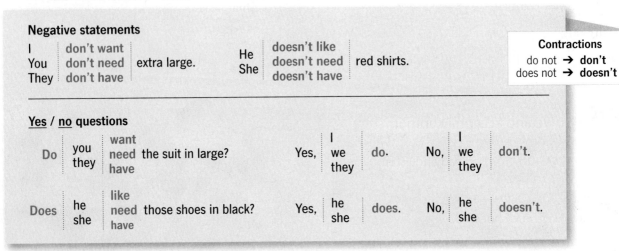

Negative statements

I	don't want		He	doesn't like	
You	don't need	extra large.	She	doesn't need	red shirts.
They	don't have			doesn't have	

Contractions
do not → **don't**
does not → **doesn't**

Yes / no questions

Do	you they	want need have	the suit in large?	Yes,	I we they	do.	No,	I we they	don't.
Does	he she	like need have	those shoes in black?	Yes,	he she	does.	No,	he she	doesn't.

4 GRAMMAR PRACTICE Complete the sentences with the correct form of the verb. Use contractions.

1 A: .....*Do*.... your children ...*have*... sweaters for
      school?
       have

   B: My daughter ...*does*..., but my son ...*doesn't*. .

2 A: .... your husband .... a black tie?
                                           need

   B: No, he .... He .... two black ties.
                                    have

3 A: I .... a blue suit for work. .... you
          need

      .... one too?
         need

   B: Yes, I ....

4 A: .... you .... that green
                              like
      shirt?

   B: Actually, no, I ....

5 A: We .... the clothes in this store.
              not like

   B: Really? That's too bad. We ....

6 A: .... you .... this black jacket in
      size 34?   *have*

   B: No, I'm sorry. We ....

5 ▶2:42 **LISTENING COMPREHENSION** Listen to the conversations about clothes. Check each statement T (true) or F (false). Then listen again and circle the color.

T F
☐ ☐ **1** They like the dress.

☐ ☐ **2** He needs shoes.

☐ ☐ **3** Matt needs a suit for work.

T F
☐ ☐ **4** He needs a tie.

☐ ☐ **5** She needs the sweater in small.

☐ ☐ **6** They don't have his size.

NOW YOU CAN **Ask for colors and sizes**

1 ▶2:43 **CONVERSATION MODEL** Read and listen.

A: Do you have this sweater in green?
B: Yes, we do.

A: Great. And my husband needs a shirt. Do you have that shirt in large?
B: No, I'm sorry. We don't.
A: That's too bad.

▶2:44 **RHYTHM AND INTONATION** Listen again and repeat. Then practice the Conversation Model with a partner.

CONVERSATION ACTIVATOR With a partner, change the conversation. Ask for colors and sizes of clothes for you and a relative. Use the pictures. Then change roles.

A: Do you have .... in ....?
B: ....
A: .... And my .... needs .... Do you have .... in ....?
B: ....
A: ....

CHANGE PARTNERS Practice the conversation again. Ask about other clothes.

1 ▶ 2:45 **VOCABULARY** • *Opposite adjectives to describe clothes* Read and listen. Then listen again and repeat.

1 new

2 old

3 dirty   **4** clean

9 long   **10** short

5 loose

6 tight

7 cheap

8 expensive

2 GRAMMAR • *Adjective placement*

> **Adjectives come before the nouns they describe.**
> a **long** skirt   **tight** shoes   a **red** and **black** tie
>
> **Adjectives don't change.**
> a **clean** shirt / **clean** shirts   NOT   ~~cleans~~ shirts
>
> **Place _very_ before adjectives.**
> The skirt is **very** long. It's a **very** long skirt.

> **Be careful!**
> It's a **long skirt**.
> NOT It's a ~~skirt long~~.

3 **PAIR WORK** Look at your classmates. Take turns describing their clothes.

> ❝ Allen has new shoes ❞

> ❝ Joe's shoes are old.
> He needs new shoes. ❞

4 **GRAMMAR PRACTICE** Write two descriptions for each picture. Follow the model.

1 The ....*blouses*.. are ....*clean*......
They're ....*clean blouses*.......... .

3 The .... are very ....
They're very ....

2 The .... is ....
It's ....

GRAMMAR • *The simple present tense: questions with <u>What</u>, <u>What color</u>, <u>What size</u>, <u>Why</u>, and <u>Which</u> / <u>One</u> and <u>ones</u>*

> Use a question word and <u>do</u> or <u>does</u> to ask information questions in the simple present tense.
> What **do** you **need**? (A blue and white tie.)   What **does** she **want**? (New shoes.)
>
> Use <u>because</u> to answer questions with <u>Why</u>.
> Why **do** they **want** that suit? (**Because** it's nice.)   Why **does** he **like** this tie? (**Because** it's green.)
>
> Use <u>What color</u> and <u>What size</u> to ask about color and size.
> What color **do** you **want**? (Black.)   What size **does** he **need**? (Extra large.)
>
> Use <u>Which</u> to ask about choice. Answer with <u>one</u> or <u>ones</u>.
> Which sweater **do** you **want**? (The blue **one**.)   Which shoes **does** she **like**? (The black **ones**.)

6 GRAMMAR PRACTICE Complete the conversations in your own words. Then practice with a partner.

1 A: Which skirt ....?
                              she / want
  B: The .... one.

2 A: What ....?
                your friend / need
  B: ....

3 A: What color shoes ....?
                             you / like
  B: ....

4 A: Why .... new shoes?
                 you / want
  B: ....

5 A: Which shirts ....?
                   you / like
  B: The .... ones.

6 A: What size shoes ....?
                   you / need
  B: ....

NOW YOU CAN Describe clothes

▶2:46 **CONVERSATION MODEL** Read and listen.

A: What do you think of this jacket?
B: I think it's nice. What about you?
A: Well, it's nice, but it's a little tight.
B: Let's keep looking.

▶2:47 **RHYTHM AND INTONATION** Listen again and repeat. Then practice the Conversation Model with a partner.

CONVERSATION ACTIVATOR With a partner, change the conversation. Use different clothes and problems. Then change roles.

A: What do you think of .... ?
B: I think .... nice. What about you?
A: Well, ... nice, but .... a little ....
B: Let's keep looking.

RECYCLE THIS LANGUAGE.

Clothes		Problems
shirt	pants	expensive
sweater	skirt	tight
dress	jacket	loose
tie	shoes	long
		short

CHANGE PARTNERS Talk about different clothes and problems.

EXTENSION

1 ▶ 2:48 **READING** Read the advertisement from today's newspaper. Which clothes do you like?

Smith and Company

TODAY ONLY!
1/2 Price Sale

Low, Low Prices!

A Great Clothes Store!
Men's and Women's Clothes
All stores open until midnight

*Blue at Main Street store only.

* White not available at South Street Station location.

Many more shoe styles available.

Other sale items today: Children's jackets and shoes

STORE LOCATIONS: 62 MAIN STREET, THE UPTOWN MALL, AND SOUTH STREET STATION

2 **READING COMPREHENSION** Read the statements about the advertisement. Check <u>True</u> or <u>False</u>.

	True	False
1 The sale is every day this week.	☐	☐
2 The store has three locations.	☐	☐
3 Smith and Company is a clothes store.	☐	☐

	True	False
4 White blouses are on sale at two locations.	☐	☐
5 All locations have blue sweaters.	☐	☐
6 Smith and Company doesn't have children's shoes.	☐	☐

DIGITAL
MORE
EXERCISES

3 **PAIR WORK** Discuss the sale at Smith and Company. Use the advertisement.

❝ What do you need? ❞

❝ I need a white blouse, and my sister needs shoes for school. Let's go to Smith and Company. They have a great sale. ❞

RECYCLE THIS LANGUAGE.
Do you want ___ ?
Do you like this / that ___ ?
Do you need [a gray tie]?
What do you need / like / want / have?
Which ___ do you ___ ?
Why do you ___ these / those ___ ?

GRAMMAR BOOSTER
Unit 6 review • p. 139

GAME Describe people's clothes. Your partner points to the picture. For example: *He has a yellow shirt.*

PAIR WORK

1 Create conversations for the people in the store. For example:
   A: *Do you want these pants?*   B: *No, I don't.*

2 Point to the picture. Ask and answer questions. Use <u>this</u> / <u>that</u> / <u>these</u> / <u>those</u> and <u>like</u>, <u>want</u>, <u>need</u>, and <u>have</u>. For example:
   A: *Do you like these shoes?*   B: *Yes, I do.*

WRITING Write about clothes you need, you want, and you like, and about clothes you have or don't have. For example:

> *I need a new white blouse. My old blouse is a*
> *little tight. I want red shoes and a long skirt . . .*

WRITING BOOSTER p. 147
Guidance for this writing exercise

NOW I CAN
☐ Give and accept a compliment.
☐ Ask for colors and sizes.
☐ Describe clothes.

LESSON 1

GOAL Talk about morning and evening activities

 DIGITAL FLASH CARDS

1 ▶ 3:02 VOCABULARY • *Daily activities at home* Read and listen. Then listen again and repeat.

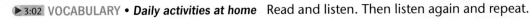

1 get up **2** get dressed **3** brush my teeth **4** comb / brush my hair **5** shave

6 put on makeup **7** eat breakfast **8** come home **9** make dinner **10** study

11 watch TV **12** get undressed **13** take a shower / a bath **14** go to bed

2 **PAIR WORK** Tell your partner about your daily activities.

❝ I eat lunch at 12:00. ❞

▶ 3:03 **Meals**
breakfast
lunch
dinner

3 **GRAMMAR** • *The simple present tense: spelling rules with he, she, and it*

Add -s to the base form of most verbs.
gets   shaves   combs

Add -es to verbs that end in -s, -sh, -ch, or -x.
brushes   watches

Remember:
do → does
go → goes
have → has
study → studies

4 VOCABULARY / GRAMMAR PRACTICE Complete the statements. Use the simple present tense.

1 Ed .... up at 6:00, but his
   get
   wife, Amy, ... up at 7:00.
   get

2 Amy .... breakfast at 7:30 A.M.,
   eat
   but Ed .... breakfast at 6:30.
   eat

3 After breakfast, Ed .... , and Amy
   shave
   .... on makeup.
   put

4 Ed and Amy .... TV in the evening.
   watch

5 Amy .... to bed at 10:00 P.M.,
   go
   but Ed .... to bed at 11:00.
   go

6 Amy .... dinner on weekdays,
   make
   and Ed .... dinner on weekends.
   make

7 Ed .... a shower in the morning,
   take
   but Amy .... a bath.
   take

8 They both .... their teeth in the
   brush
   morning and the evening.

GRAMMAR • *The simple present tense: questions with __When__ and __What time__*

> When **do you take** a shower? (In the morning.)
> What time **does** she **get** up? (Before 7:00 A.M.)

before 8:00 `7:45` | after 8:00 `8:15`

GRAMMAR PRACTICE Write five questions
about Ed and Amy. Answer your partner's
questions aloud.

1 When does Ed shave?

❝ He shaves after
breakfast. ❞

IOW YOU CAN Talk about morning and evening activities

▶3:04 CONVERSATION MODEL Read and listen.

A: Are you a morning person or an evening person?
B: Me? I'm definitely an evening person.
A: And why do you say that?
B: Well, I get up after ten in the morning. And I go to bed
   after two. What about you?
A: I'm a morning person. I get up before six.

▶3:05 RHYTHM AND INTONATION Listen again and repeat.
Then practice the Conversation Model with a partner.

CONVERSATION ACTIVATOR With a partner, personalize the
conversation. Use your own information.

A: Are you a morning person or an evening person?
B: Me? I'm definitely ....
A: And why do you say that?
B: Well, I .... What about you?
A: I'm .... I ....

DON'T STOP!
Ask more questions.

CHANGE PARTNERS Personalize
the conversation again.

RECYCLE THIS LANGUAGE.
When do you ___?
What time do you ___?
What about your [parents]?

CLASS SURVEY Find out how many students are
morning people and how many are evening people.

GOAL Describe what you do in your free time

1 ▶ 3:06 VOCABULARY • *Leisure activities* Read and listen. Then listen again and repeat.

1 exercise

2 take a nap

3 listen to music

4 read

5 play soccer

6 check e-mail

7 go out for dinner

8 go to the movies

9 go dancing

10 visit friends

2 VOCABULARY / GRAMMAR PRACTICE Write six questions for a classmate about his or her leisure activities. Use <u>When</u> or <u>What time</u> and the simple present tense.

1 When do you visit friends?

1	4
2	5
3	6

3 GRAMMAR • *The simple present tense: frequency adverbs*

100% I **always** play soccer on Saturday.
I **usually** check e-mail in the evening.
I **sometimes** go dancing on weekends.
0% I **never** take a nap in the afternoon.

Be careful!
Place the frequency adverb before the verb in the simple present tense.

Don't say: I ~~play always~~ soccer.
He ~~checks usually~~ e-mail.

4 PAIR WORK Now use your questions from Exercise 2 to ask your partner about leisure activities. Use frequency adverbs and time expressions in your answers.

❝ When do you visit friends? ❞

❝ I usually visit friends on Saturday. ❞

5 GRAMMAR PRACTICE On a separate sheet of paper, write sentences about your partner from your conversation in Exercise 4.

Scott usually visits friends on Saturday.

6 GROUP WORK Tell the class about your partner's activities.

NOW YOU CAN Describe what you do in your free time

1 ▶3:07 CONVERSATION MODEL Read and listen.

A: What's your typical day like?
B: Well, I usually go to work at 9:00, and I come home at 6:00.
A: And what do you do in your free time?
B: I sometimes read or watch TV. What about you?
A: Pretty much the same.

2 ▶3:08 RHYTHM AND INTONATION Listen again and repeat. Then practice the Conversation Model with a partner.

3 CONVERSATION ACTIVATOR On the notepad, write your typical daily activities. Then, with a partner, personalize the conversation.

A: What's your typical day like?
B: Well, I ....
A: And what do you do in your free time?
B: .... What about you?
A: ....

On weekdays

On weekends

DON'T STOP!
Ask about other times and days.

 RECYCLE THIS LANGUAGE.
on [Friday]
in the morning
in the afternoon
in the evening
at night

4 CHANGE PARTNERS Personalize the conversation again.

VOCABULARY BOOSTE
More household chores • p.

DIGITAL FLASH CARDS

1 ▶ 3:09 **VOCABULARY • *Household chores*** Read and listen. Then listen again and repeat.

1 wash the dishes

2 clean the house

3 do the laundry

4 take out the garbage

5 go shopping

2 GRAMMAR • *The simple present tense: questions with How often / Other time expressions*

How often **do** you **take** out the garbage?
I take out the garbage **every day.**

M	T	W	T	F	S	S
✓	✓	✓	✓	✓	✓	✓

How often **does** she **go** shopping?
She goes shopping **on Saturdays.**

M	T	W	T	F	S	S
					✓	
					✓	

Other time expressions

	M	T	W	T	F	S	S
once a week	✓						
twice a week		✓		✓			
three times a week		✓		✓	✓		

Also
• once a year
• twice a day
• three times a month
• every weekend
• every Friday

3 PAIR WORK Ask and answer questions about chores. Use How often.

❝ How often do you go shopping? ❞

❝ Twice a week. ❞

DIGITAL VIDEO COACH

4 ▶ 3:10 **PRONUNCIATION • *Third-person singular verb endings*** Read and listen.
Then listen again and repeat.

1 /s/	**2** /z/	**3** /ɪz/
take**s** = take/s/	clean**s** = clean/z/	wash**es** = wash/ɪz/
visit**s** = visit/s/	doe**s** = doe/z/	practic**es** = practice/ɪz/
eat**s** = eat/s/	play**s** = play/z/	exercis**es** = exercise/ɪz/

DIGITAL MORE EXERCISES

5 VOCABULARY / GRAMMAR PRACTICE Tell your class how often your partner from Exercise 3
does household chores. Practice pronunciation of third-person verb endings.

❝ John **goes** shopping twice a week. ❞

6 GRAMMAR • *The simple present tense: questions with Who as subject*

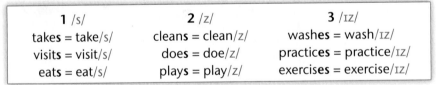

Who **washes** the dishes in your family? I do. / My sister does.
We do. / My grandparents do.

Be careful!
Always use a third-person singular verb when who is the subject.
Don't say: Who ~~wash~~ the dishes?

Don't use do or does when who is the subject.
Don't say: Who ~~does wash~~ the dishes?

▶3:11 LISTENING COMPREHENSION Listen to the conversations and the questions with <u>Who</u>. Check the chores each person does.

1	She...					
	Her husband...	✓				
	Her son...					
	Her daughter...					
2	He...					
	His brother...					
	His sister...					
3	She...					
	Her husband...					
4	He...					
	His wife...					
	His son...					

GRAMMAR PRACTICE With a partner, ask and answer questions about the people in Exercise 7.

> In Conversation 1, who washes the dishes?

> Her husband does.

NOW YOU CAN Discuss household chores

▶3:12 CONVERSATION MODEL Read and listen.

A: So how often do you do the laundry?
B: About twice a week. How about you?
A: Me? I never do the laundry. Could I ask another question?
B: Sure.
A: Who cleans the house?
B: Oh, that's my brother's job.

▶3:13 RHYTHM AND INTONATION Listen again and repeat. Then practice the Conversation Model with a partner.

CONVERSATION ACTIVATOR With a partner, personalize the conversation. Then change roles.

A: So how often do you .... ?
B: .... How about you?
A: Me? .... Could I ask another question?
B: ....
A: Who .... ?
B: Oh, that's .... job.

DON'T STOP!
Ask about other chores.

4 **CHANGE PARTNERS** Ask another classmate about household chores.

5 **GROUP WORK** Tell your classmates about your partner's household chores.

1 ▶ 3:14 READING Read the article. Do you like housework?

Don't like household chores?
These robots help! ▶

How often do you clean your house? Once a week? Twice a month? Never? Well, these two robots clean the house for you. The iRobot Roomba® turns right or left, and vacuums while you watch TV or exercise. Take a nap, and the house is clean when you get up. And if you want to wash the floor, the iRobot Scooba® washes the floor for you. The Scooba moves around corners and washes the floor while you listen to music or check your e-mail. Now <u>that's</u> help with household chores!

The iRobot Roomba vacuums.

The Scooba washes floors.

And who is this? Meet ASIMO, a robot from the Honda Motor Company. ASIMO doesn't clean the house. It doesn't wash dishes or take out the garbage. But ASIMO walks, climbs stairs, carries things, and pushes things. ASIMO talks, answers questions, and follows directions. Ask, "What's your name?" and ASIMO says, "I'm ASIMO." Say "turn left" or "turn right," and ASIMO turns. ASIMO also greets people. Some people think ASIMO is very cute.

ASIMO carries a tray.

ASIMO climbs stairs...

and pushes things.

2 READING COMPREHENSION Complete each statement. Circle the correct verb.

1 The Roomba (washes / vacuums / carries things).

2 The Scooba (washes / vacuums / carries things).

3 The Roomba and the Scooba (answer questions / talk / turn).

4 ASIMO (cleans / washes the floor / greets people).

5 ASIMO doesn't (clean things / carry things / talk).

6 ASIMO also (vacuums / takes out the garbage / climbs stairs).

7 ASIMO (asks / answers / repeats) questions.

8 (The Roomba / The Scooba / ASIMO) pushes things.

DIGITAL
MORE
EXERCISES

3 DISCUSSION Which robots do you like? Do you want any of them? Why?

❝ I want the Roomba because it cleans the house. ❞

GRAMMAR BOOSTE
Unit 7 review • p. 139

For additional language practice...

♫ TOP NOTCH **POP** • Lyrics p. 1
"On the Weekend"

DIGITAL
SONG

DIGITAL
KARAOKE

DIGITAL GAMES

Jack's ~~pical~~ Day

Morning

 7:00 A.M.

 7:10 A.M.

 7:45 A.M.

 8:15 A.M.

 8:30 A.M.

Evening

 0 P.M.

 6:30 P.M.

 0 P.M.

 7:30 P.M.

 P.M.

 10:15 P.M.

11:00 P.M.

CONTEST Study the photos for one minute. Then close your books. Who remembers all Jack's activities?

PAIR WORK Create a conversation for Jack and a friend. Start like this:

Jack, are you a morning person or an evening person? OR
What's your typical day like?

TRUE OR FALSE? Make statements about Jack's activities. Your partner says <u>True</u> or <u>False</u>. Take turns. For example:

A: Jack usually takes a shower in the evening.
B: False. He takes a shower in the morning.

WRITING Write about <u>your</u> typical week. Use adverbs of frequency and time expressions. For example:

In the morning, I usually eat breakfast at 7:00. Then I ...

WRITING BOOSTER p.148
Guidance for this writing exercise

✓ NOW I CAN

☐ Talk about morning and evening activities.
☐ Describe what I do in my free time.
☐ Discuss household chores.

Units 1–7 REVIEW

1 ▶ **3:17** LISTENING COMPREHENSION Listen to the conversations. Check each statement T (true) or F (false). Then listen again and check your work.

T F
- ☐ ☐ **1** The woman is a manager.
- ☐ ☐ **2** His father is a doctor.
- ☐ ☐ **3** Her sister is an architect.

T F
- ☐ ☐ **4** His brother is a student.
- ☐ ☐ **5** Her grandparents are artists.
- ☐ ☐ **6** The woman in the photo is his neighbor.

2 PAIR WORK Ask and answer questions about places on the maps.

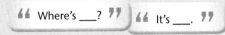

 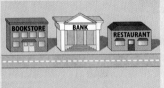  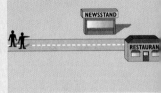

3 GRAMMAR PRACTICE Complete each sentence with <u>in</u>, <u>on</u>, or <u>at</u>.

1 The movie is .... Friday .... 8:00.

2 The meeting is .... June 6th .... the morning.

3 The party is .... Saturday .... midnight.

4 The dinner is .... April.

5 The dance is .... 8:00 P.M. .... Friday.

4 GRAMMAR PRACTICE Complete the sentences with <u>this</u>, <u>that</u>, <u>these</u>, or <u>those</u>.

 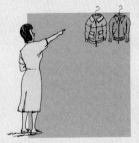  

1 I want .... pants.

2 I like .... jackets.

3 I like .... suit.

4 I want .... tie.

5 PAIR WORK

Partner A: Ask these questions.
Partner B: Read the correct response to each question aloud.

1 Does he have grandchildren?
  a Yes, he has two sons.
  b Yes, he does.

2 Where's the pharmacy?
  a Don't walk. Take the bus.
  b It's around the corner.

3 Are we late?
  a Yes. It's 10:00.
  b Yes, you're early.

Partner B: Ask these questions.
Partner A: Read the correct response to each question aloud.

4 When's the dance?
  a On Saturday.
  b At the school.

5 Do you like this suit?
  a Yes, it is.
  b Yes, I do.

6 How do you go to work?
  a I walk.
  b Walk.

6 PAIR WORK Write your own response to each person. Then practice your conversations with a partner.

1 (YOU) *Nice to meet you* .

2 (YOU) .

3 (YOU) .

4 (YOU) .

5 (YOU) .

6 (YOU) .

GRAMMAR PRACTICE Look at the pictures. Write an imperative for each.

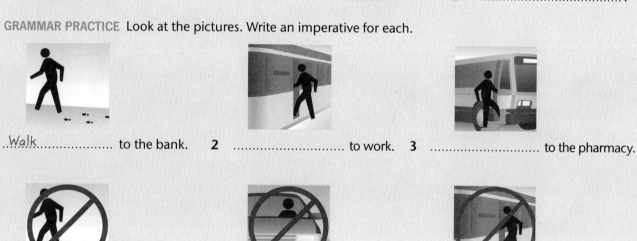

..*Walk*.......... to the bank. 2 .... to work. 3 .... to the pharmacy.

.... to the restaurant. 5 .... to school. 6 .... to the bookstore.

8 CONVERSATION PRACTICE With a partner, exchange real information about your families. Start like this:

❝ Tell me about your family. ❞

Ideas
Ask about names.   Ask about occupations.
Ask about ages.   Describe people.

9 ▶ 3:18 LISTENING COMPREHENSION Listen to the conversations. Answer the questions. Then listen again and check your work.

1	What's her phone number?	It's __ __ __ __ __ __ __ __ __ __ .
2	What's his last name?	It's __ __ __ __ __ __ .
3	How old is his son?	He's __ years old.
4	What's the address?	It's __ __ West 12th Street.
5	What time is it?	It's 2:__ __ .

10 GRAMMAR PRACTICE Circle the correct word or words to complete each statement or question.

1 Is he (your / you) husband?

2 Is she (their / they) granddaughter?

3 (Her / His) name is Mr. Grant.

4 (Our / We) birthdays are in May.

5 How do you spell (her / she) name?

6 I'm (Ms. Bell / Ms. Bell's) student.

11 VOCABULARY / GRAMMAR PRACTICE Write a question for each response.

1 **A:** .... ?
  B: No. She's a student.

2 **A:** .... ?
  B: I'm an architect.

3 **A:** .... ?
  B: The bank is across the street.

4 **A:** .... ?
  B: It's 9:45.

5 **A:** .... ?
  B: It's 34 Bank Street.

6 **A:** .... ?
  B: The newsstand is around the corner.

7 **A:** .... ?
  B: My birthday? In February.

8 **A:** .... ?
  B: They're my sisters.

12 PAIR WORK

Partner A: Ask these questions.
Partner B: Read the correct response to each question aloud.

1 Does Jack have a large family?
  a Yes, I do.
  b Yes, he does.

2 Does her father shave every morning?
  a Yes, he is.
  b No, he doesn't.

3 Is Ms. Wang his English teacher?
  a Yes, he is.
  b Yes, she is.

Partner B: Ask these questions.
Partner A: Read the correct response to each question aloud.

4 Does she like red shoes?
  a No, she doesn't.
  b Yes, I do.

5 Does he need a new tie?
  a Yes, he does.
  b Yes, I do.

6 Does she always clean the house on Sunday?
  a Yes, she is.
  b Yes, she does.

13 GRAMMAR PRACTICE Circle the correct verb to complete each sentence.

1 We (am / are) friends.

2 They (has / have) two children.

3 Who (has / have) a blue suit?

4 (Do / Does) she (want / wants) new shoes?

5 Why (do / does) they (need / needs) new shoes

6 (Is / Are) we on time?

14 GRAMMAR PRACTICE Complete the statements with verbs in the simple present tense.

1 I usually .... TV in the evening, but my brother .... to music.

2 We sometimes .... the house and .... the laundry in the morning.

3 After dinner, I always .... the dishes, and my wife .... out the garbage.

4 My neighbors never .... shopping on weekdays.

5 My sister always .... to bed before 10:00 P.M., but I usually .... e-mail at 10:00.

6 My grandfather always .... a nap in the afternoon.

15 VOCABULARY / GRAMMAR PRACTICE Answer the questions. Use frequency adverbs or time expressions. Then tell your classmates about your activities.

1 What do you do on weekends?

> 1 I usually go shopping on weekends.

2 What do you do after breakfast?

3 What do you do after work or school?

4 What do you do at night before you go to bed?

16 CONVERSATION PRACTICE With a partner, talk about the times of events. Use the pictures or your own ideas. Start like this:

> " Look. There's a _____ on _____ . "

RECYCLE THIS LANGUAGE.

Really?
What time?
Let's go!
Good idea.

across the street
down the street
around the corner

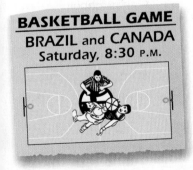

Other events
a meeting
a party
a dance
a dinner
(your own idea)

UNIT **8** Home and Neighborhood

COMMUNICATION GOALS

1 Describe your neighborhood.
2 Ask about someone's home.
3 Talk about furniture and appliances.

LESSON **1** **GOAL** Describe your neighborhood

DIGITAL FLASH CARDS

1 ▶ 3:19 VOCABULARY • *Buildings* Read and listen. Then listen again and repeat.

1 A HOUSE

4 a garden
5 a garage

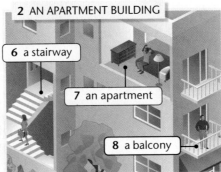

2 AN APARTMENT BUILDING

6 a stairway
7 an apartment
8 a balcony

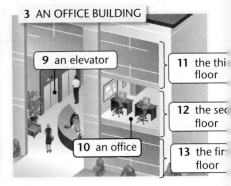

3 AN OFFICE BUILDING

9 an elevator
10 an office
11 the thi... floor
12 the se... floor
13 the fir... floor

2 GRAMMAR • *The simple present tense: questions with* <u>Where</u> */ Prepositions of place*

Questions with <u>Where</u>

Where **do** you **live**?
Where **do** your parents **live**?

Where **does** he **work**?
Where **does** your mother **work**?

Prepositions of place

in
She lives **in** an apartment.
They live **in** a house.
I work **in** an office.

at
I live **at** 50 Main Street.
He works **at** a bookstore.
They study **at** the Brooke School.

on
Her house is **on** Bank Street.
We go to school **on** 34th Avenue.
I work **on** the tenth floor.

3 GRAMMAR PRACTICE Complete the conversations. Use the simple present tense and prepositions of place.

1 **A:** Where .... your sister .... ?
   B: She lives .... an apartment.

2 **A:** Where .... you .... English?
   B: We study .... the school around the corner.

3 **A:** Where .... your neighbor ....
   B: She works .... a bookstore.

4 **A:** Where .... your parents ....
   B: They live .... 58 Gray Street.

DIGITAL MORE EXERCISES

DIGITAL VIDEO COACH

4 ▶ 3:20 PRONUNCIATION • *Linking sounds* Read and listen. Then listen and repeat.

1 It's on the second floor.

2 She works in an office.

3 He lives in an apartment.

4 My apartment has a balcony.

5 VOCABULARY / GRAMMAR PRACTICE With a partner, ask and answer questions with <u>Where</u>. Use the simple present tense.

6 ▶ 3:21 VOCABULARY • *Places in the neighborhood* Read and listen. Then listen again and repeat.

1 a bus station   **2** a train station   **3** a stadium

▶ 3:22 Preposition <u>near</u>

Train Station

Bus Station

The train station is **near** the bus station. It's right across the street.

4 a park   **5** a mall   **6** a museum   **7** an airport   **8** a hospital

NOW YOU CAN Describe your neighborhood

▶ 3:23 CONVERSATION MODEL Read and listen.

A: Do you live far from here?
B: No. About fifteen minutes by bus.
A: And is the neighborhood nice?
B: Yes, it is. My apartment is near a park and a mall.
A: Really? My apartment is next to an airport.

▶ 3:24 RHYTHM AND INTONATION Listen again and repeat. Then practice the Conversation Model with a partner.

CONVERSATION ACTIVATOR With a partner, personalize the conversation.

A: Do you live far from here?
B: ....
A: And is the neighborhood nice?
B: ...., it .... My .... is ....
A: Really? My .... is ....

CHANGE PARTNERS Ask about another classmate's neighborhood.

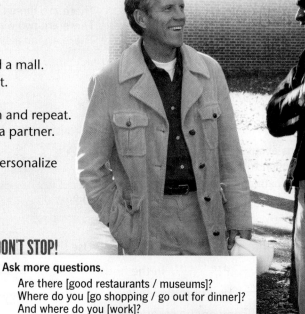

DON'T STOP!
Ask more questions.
Are there [good restaurants / museums]?
Where do you [go shopping / go out for dinner]?
And where do you [work]?

GOAL Ask about someone's home

1 ▶3:25 VOCABULARY • *Rooms* Read and listen. Then listen again and repeat.

1 upstairs
2 downstairs

3 a bathroom
4 a living room
5 a bedroom
6 a dining room
7 a kitchen
8 a door
9 a closet
10 a window

Preposition in
Use **in** for rooms.
The closet is **in** the bedroom.

2 PAIR WORK Tell your partner about the rooms in your home.

" My apartment has one large
bedroom and two small bedrooms. "

3 GRAMMAR • *There is* and *There are* / *Questions with How many*

There is and There are
Use **There is** with singular nouns. Use **There are** with plural nouns.

There's a small bedroom downstairs.
There's a large closet and two windows.
There's no kitchen.

Is there a balcony? | Yes, there is.
| No, there isn't.

There are three large bedrooms upstairs.
There are two windows and a large closet.
There are no elevators.

Are there closets? | Yes, there are.
| No, there aren't.

Be careful!
There is → **There's**
BUT Yes, there is. NOT Yes, ~~there's~~.
There are NOT ~~There're~~

How many
Ask questions about quantity with **How many**. Always
use a plural noun with **How many**.

How many bathrooms **are there**? (There are two.)
How many bedrooms **do you have**? (We have three.)

4 GRAMMAR PRACTICE Complete the sentences. Use there's, there are, is there, or are there.

1 How many closets *are there* in the house?
2 .... a small bedroom downstairs.
3 .... a balcony on the second floor?
4 .... an elevator and two stairways.

5 .... a garden next to her house.
6 .... two bedrooms upstairs.
7 .... a park near my apartment.
8 How many windows ....?

5 GRAMMAR PRACTICE Write ten sentences about your house or apartment. Use <u>There is</u> and <u>There are</u>.

> There's a small bathroom next to my bedroom.

Ideas
• number of rooms
• size of rooms
• location of rooms

6 ▶3:26 LISTENING COMPREHENSION Listen to the conversations. Check the best house or apartment for each person.

http://www.homeawayfromhome.com

Home Away from Home
Live in a house or apartment overseas for 1 to 6 months!
Call Us at 1-800-555-9038

1. Paris
☐ A two-bedroom house with a large kitchen
☐ A one-bedroom apartment with a small kitchen

2. Buenos Aires
☐ A two-bedroom house with three bathrooms
☐ A two-bedroom house with two bathrooms

3. Tokyo
☐ A one-bedroom apartment with a large kitchen
☐ A one-bedroom apartment with a large closet

4. Montreal
☐ A two-bedroom house with a small garden
☐ A two-bedroom apartment with a balcony

IOW YOU CAN Ask about someone's home

▶3:27 CONVERSATION MODEL Read and listen.

A: Do you live in a house or an apartment?
B: An apartment.
A: What's it like?
B: Well, there are three large bedrooms, and it has a large kitchen.
A: Sounds nice!

▶3:28 RHYTHM AND INTONATION Listen again and repeat. Then practice the Conversation Model with a partner.

CONVERSATION ACTIVATOR With a partner, personalize the conversation. Describe your house or apartment. Then change roles.

A: Do you live in a house or an apartment?
B: ....
A: What's it like?
B: Well, ...
A: Sounds nice!

DON'T STOP!
Ask more questions.
Is there ___ ? / Are there ___ ?
How many ___ are there?
Does your [house] have [a garage]?

CHANGE PARTNERS Talk about another classmate's home.

1 ▶3:29 VOCABULARY • *Furniture and appliances* First write the name of each room (a–f). Then read and listen. Listen again and repeat.

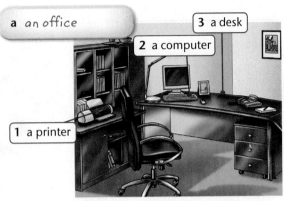

a *an office*
3 a desk
2 a computer
1 a printer

b
7 a lamp
5 a bed
4 a dresser
6 a rug

c
10 a shower
9 a mirror
11 a sink
8 a toilet
12 a bathtub

d
13 a table
14 a chair

e
16 a bookcase
15 a sofa
17 a TV

f
18 a cabinet
20 a microwave
21 a stove
19 a refrigerator (a fridge)

VOCABULARY BOOSTER
More home and office vocabulary • p. 12

2 ▶3:30 LISTENING COMPREHENSION Listen to the comments about furniture and appliances. Look at the pictures in the Vocabulary. Write the correct room.

1 It's in the ....
2 It's in the ....
3 It's in the ....
4 It's in the ....
5 They're in the ....
6 It's in the ....

3 PAIR WORK Ask your partner about the furniture and appliances in his or her home.

> " What's in your living room? "

> " My living room has a sofa and two chairs, and there's a large bookcase. "

NOW YOU CAN | Talk about furniture and appliances

▶ 3:31 **CONVERSATION MODEL** Read and listen.

A: This is a nice sofa. What do you think?
B: Actually, I think it's beautiful.
A: And what about this lamp?
B: I don't know. I'm not sure.

▶ 3:32 **RHYTHM AND INTONATION** Listen again and repeat. Then practice the Conversation Model with a partner.

CONVERSATION ACTIVATOR Change the conversation. Ask your partner's opinion about the furniture and appliances in the pictures. (Or use your own pictures.) Then change roles.

A: This is a nice .... What do you think?
B: Actually, I think it's ....
A: And what about this .... ?
B: ....

DON'T STOP!
Ask about other furniture and appliances.

> ▶ 3:33
> **Positive and negative adjectives**
> ☺   ☹
> beautiful   ugly
> nice   awful
> great   terrible

🔁 **RECYCLE THIS LANGUAGE.**
I like this ___ .
I don't like this ___ .
Really?
What about you?

CHANGE PARTNERS Practice the conversation again.

1   ▶ 3:34 READING   Read about where people live. Who lives in a house?
Who lives in an apartment?

Where Do You Live?

Jeewhan Yoon

Tina Williams

Eduardo Calero

I'm Jeewhan Yoon from the city of Busan, in Korea. My wife and I live in a small house with two floors and a garage. There are two bedrooms, a living room, a small kitchen, and one bathroom.

My favorite room is the living room. There's a big sofa, and I usually read there. We also watch movies on TV in the living room.

One thing I don't like: we don't have a garden.

I'm Tina Williams, and I'm from Seattle, in the United States. I live in a small white house with a two-car garage.

Downstairs, there's a living room, a dining room, and a nice large kitchen with large windows and a view of the garden. There are two bedrooms and one bathroom upstairs. There's also a very small office—my favorite room. I study there.

It's small, but I love my house!

My name is Eduardo Calero, and I live in Caracas, Venezuela. My family has a really nice apartment on the eighth floor. There's an elevator, of course, and there's a garage on the first floor.

We have three bedrooms and two bathrooms. My brother and I have our own rooms. The kitchen is small, but it has beautiful new appliances. The living room is my favorite room, though, because it has a fantastic view of the city of Caracas.

2   READING COMPREHENSION   Check the descriptions that match each person's home.

	Jeewhan Yoon	Tina Williams	Eduardo Calero
three bedrooms	☐	☐	☐
two bathrooms	☐	☐	☐
a small kitchen	☐	☐	☐
no office	☐	☐	☐
no garden	☐	☐	☐
a two-car garage	☐	☐	☐
an elevator	☐	☐	☐

3   PAIR WORK   Compare your home with the homes in the Reading.

66 Tina's kitchen has a view of the garden, but my house doesn't have a garden. 99

66 Eduardo lives in an apartment. I live in an apartment, too. His apartment has two bathrooms, but my apartment has one. 99

GRAMMAR BOOSTER
Unit 8 review • p. 140

For additional language practice . . .

♫ TOP NOTCH POP   • Lyrics p. 1[
"Home Is Where the Heart Is"

Partner A's Picture

INFO GAP Find everything that's different in the two pictures. Ask questions. For example:

How many __ are there? Is there __?
Does the __ have __? Are there __?

PAIR WORK

1 Express your opinions about the houses, the furniture, and the appliances. For example:
A: What do you think of __?
B: I think it's really nice. What about you?

2 Your partner closes his or her book. You describe one of the houses. Your partner draws a picture of the house. For example:
Upstairs, there are two small bedrooms and a small bathroom.

WRITING Compare your home with one of the homes in the Reading on page 70. For example:

Ms. Williams's house has two bedrooms upstairs, but my...

WRITING BOOSTER p. 148
Guidance for this writing exercise

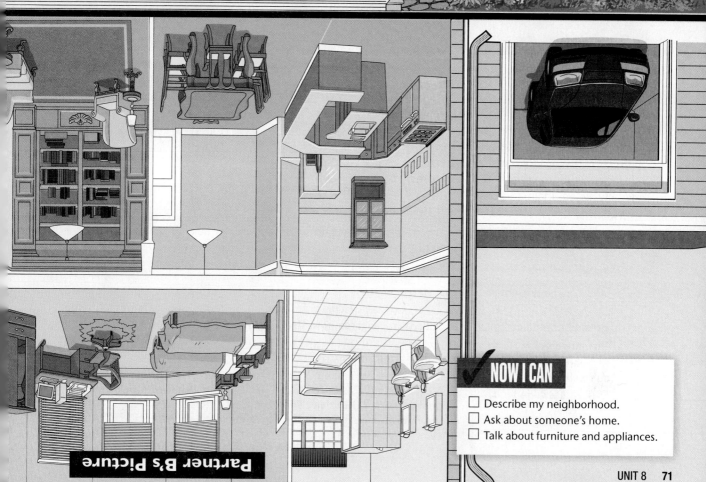

Partner B's Picture

✔ **NOW I CAN**

☐ Describe my neighborhood.
☐ Ask about someone's home.
☐ Talk about furniture and appliances.

UNIT 9 Activities and Plans

LESSON 1

GOAL Describe today's weather

VOCABULARY BOOSTER
More weather vocabulary • p. 130

1 ▶ 3:37 VOCABULARY • *Weather expressions* Read and listen. Then listen again and repeat.

DIGITAL FLASH CARDS

HOW'S THE WEATHER?

1 It's sunny.

2 It's cloudy.

6 It's hot.

7 It's cold.

3 It's windy.

4 It's raining.

5 It's snowing.

8 It's warm.

9 It's cool.

2 ▶ 3:38 LISTENING COMPREHENSION
Listen to the weather reports. Check the correct word for each city. Then listen again and write the temperatures. Finally, listen again and describe the weather.

City	Hot	Warm	Cool	Cold	What's the temperature?	How's the weather?
1 Cali	✓				35°	It's sunny
2 Madrid						
3 Seoul						
4 Dubai						
5 Montreal						

3 GRAMMAR • *The present continuous: statements*

The present continuous expresses actions in progress now. Use a form of <u>be</u> and a present participle.

Affirmative
I'm wearing a sweater.
You're shaving.
She's taking a bath.
It's raining.
We're watching TV.
They're exercising.

Negative
I'm not wearing a jacket.
You're not making lunch. [OR You aren't making lunch.]
She's not taking a shower. [OR She isn't taking a shower.]
It's not snowing. [OR It isn't snowing.]
We're not reading. [OR We aren't reading.]
They're not taking a nap. [OR They aren't taking a nap.]

Present participles
wear → wearing
study → studying
exercise → exercising

Some others:
doing, listening, reading, working, meeting, getting

4

GRAMMAR • *The present continuous: <u>yes</u> / <u>no</u> questions*

Are you eating right now?	Yes, I am. / No, I'm not.
Is she taking the bus?	Yes, she is. / No, she's not. [OR No, she isn't.]
Is it raining?	Yes, it is. / No, it's not. [OR No, it isn't.]
Are they walking?	Yes, they are. / No, they're not. [OR No, they aren't.]

GRAMMAR PRACTICE Complete each statement, question, or short answer with the present continuous. Use contractions.

1 .... now, and .... a nice, warm sweater.
    It / snow   I / wear

2 ....? Yes, he .... his textbook.
    he /study   He / read

3 .... dinner right now. .... late at the office.
    Dad / not make   He / work

4 .... , and .... a shower.
    Jerome / exercise   Ann / take

5 .... TV. .... to music.
    The children / not watch   They / listen

6 .... this morning? No. It's cloudy and windy, but it ....
    it /rain   not rain

7 .... in the office right now? Yes, ...
    they / meet

NOW YOU CAN Describe today's weather

▶ 3:39 **CONVERSATION MODEL** Read and listen.

A: Hi, Molly. Jonathan.
B: Hey, Jonathan. Where are you?
A: I'm calling from Vancouver.
   How's the weather there in São Paulo?
B: Today? Awful! It's raining and cold.
A: No kidding! It's hot and sunny here.

bad ☹
Awful!
Terrible!

good ☺
Nice!
Great!
Beautiful!

▶ 3:40 **RHYTHM AND INTONATION** Listen again and repeat. Then practice the Conversation Model with a partner.

CONVERSATION ACTIVATOR With a partner, change the conversation. Choose two cities. Role-play a conversation about the weather there. (Option: Find the weather report in the newspaper, on TV, or online.) Then change roles.

A: Hi, ...
B: .... , ... Where are you?
A: I'm calling from ....
   How's the weather there in .... ?
B: Today? .... It's ....
A: No kidding! It's .... here.

DON'T STOP!
Tell your partner what you're wearing.
  I'm wearing ___.
  I'm not wearing ___.

a scarf
a coat

CHANGE PARTNERS Describe the weather in other places.

GOAL Discuss plans

1 ▶3:41 **VOCABULARY** • *Present and future time expressions* Read and listen. Then listen again and repeat.

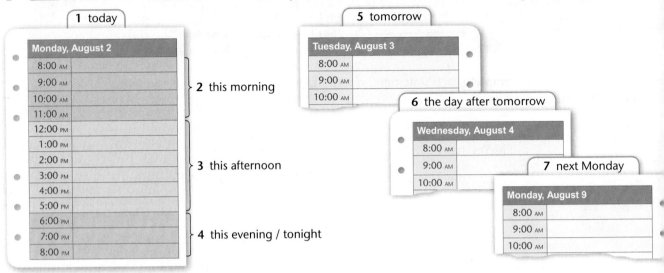

1 today

Monday, August 2

| 8:00 AM |
| 9:00 AM |
| 10:00 AM |
| 11:00 AM |
| 12:00 PM |
| 1:00 PM |
| 2:00 PM |
| 3:00 PM |
| 4:00 PM |
| 5:00 PM |
| 6:00 PM |
| 7:00 PM |
| 8:00 PM |

2 this morning

3 this afternoon

4 this evening / tonight

5 tomorrow

Tuesday, August 3

| 8:00 AM |
| 9:00 AM |
| 10:00 AM |

6 the day after tomorrow

Wednesday, August 4

| 8:00 AM |
| 9:00 AM |
| 10:00 AM |

7 next Monday

Monday, August 9

| 8:00 AM |
| 9:00 AM |
| 10:00 AM |

2 GRAMMAR • *The present continuous with present and future time expressions*

Actions in the present	Future plans
Are you watching TV **right now**? I'm not studying English **this year**. She's working at home **this week**.	I'm buying shoes **tomorrow**. They're cleaning the house **this weekend**, not today. Janet's meeting Bill **at 5:00 this afternoon**.

3 GRAMMAR PRACTICE Read Marissa Miller's date book for this week. Then complete the paragraph. Use the present continuous.

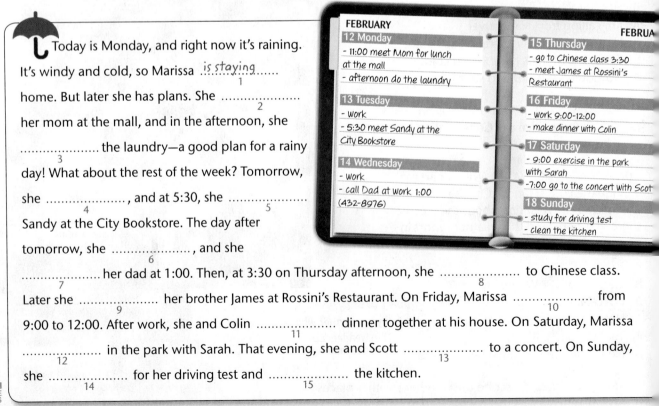

Today is Monday, and right now it's raining. It's windy and cold, so Marissa ...is staying...
1
home. But later she has plans. She ....
2
her mom at the mall, and in the afternoon, she
.... the laundry—a good plan for a rainy
3
day! What about the rest of the week? Tomorrow,
she .... , and at 5:30, she ....
4   5
Sandy at the City Bookstore. The day after
tomorrow, she .... , and she
6
.... her dad at 1:00. Then, at 3:30 on Thursday afternoon, she .... to Chinese class.
7   8
Later she .... her brother James at Rossini's Restaurant. On Friday, Marissa .... from
9   10
9:00 to 12:00. After work, she and Colin .... dinner together at his house. On Saturday, Marissa
11
.... in the park with Sarah. That evening, she and Scott .... to a concert. On Sunday,
12   13
she .... for her driving test and .... the kitchen.
14   15

FEBRUARY

12 Monday
- 11:00 meet Mom for lunch at the mall
- afternoon do the laundry

13 Tuesday
- work
- 5:30 meet Sandy at the City Bookstore

14 Wednesday
- work
- call Dad at work 1:00 (432-8976)

15 Thursday   FEBRUA
- go to Chinese class 3:30
- meet James at Rossini's Restaurant

16 Friday
- work 9:00-12:00
- make dinner with Colin

17 Saturday
- 9:00 exercise in the park with Sarah
- 7:00 go to the concert with Scot

18 Sunday
- study for driving test
- clean the kitchen

4 PAIR WORK Ask your partner <u>yes</u> / <u>no</u> questions about Marissa's schedule. Use the present continuous. Answer your partner's questions.

> " Is Marissa exercising on Tuesday? "

NOW YOU CAN Discuss plans

1 ▶3:42 **CONVERSATION MODEL** Read and listen.

A: What beautiful weather! It's so sunny and warm!
B: It really is! . . . So, Kate, are you doing anything special this weekend?
A: Well, on Saturday, I'm meeting Pam in the park.
B: Do you want to get together on Sunday?
A: Sure! Call me Sunday morning, OK?

2 ▶3:43 **RHYTHM AND INTONATION** Listen again and repeat. Then practice the Conversation Model with a partner.

3 **PLAN YOUR CONVERSATION** Fill in the date book for this week. Write your activities and the times.

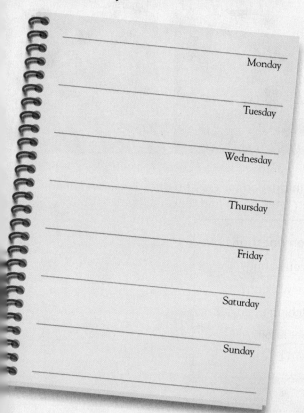

Monday

Tuesday

Wednesday

Thursday

Friday

Saturday

Sunday

DIGITAL VIDEO

4 **CONVERSATION ACTIVATOR** With a partner, personalize the conversation with real information from your date books. Describe the weather today and use the time expressions for your plans. Then change roles.

A: What .... weather! It's so .... !
B: It really is! . . . So, ..., are you doing anything special ....?
A: Well, ..., I'm ....
B: Do you want to get together .... ?
A: Sure! Call me ...., OK?

DON'T STOP!
Ask about plans for other days of the week.

 **RECYCLE THIS LANGUAGE.**

Time expressions	Adjectives for weather		Describe the weather
on [Friday]	bad	good	It's so [cloudy / windy]!
this [afternoon]	awful	nice	And it's so [hot / cold / cool]!
in the [evening]	terrible	great	And it's [raining / snowing]!
tomorrow	ugly	beautiful	
the day after tomorrow			

5 **CHANGE PARTNERS** Discuss other plans.

1 GRAMMAR • *The present continuous: information questions*

> What **is** she **watching**? (A TV program.)   What **are** you **doing**? (We're checking e-mail.)
> Where **is** he **driving**? (To work.)   Where **are** they **going**? (They're going to the movies.)
>
> **BUT: Note the different word order when <u>who</u> is the subject.**
> Who **is working**? (Ben.)

2 PAIR WORK Ask and answer questions about Mike and Patty. Use the present continuous and <u>What</u>, <u>Where</u>, and <u>Who</u>.

> 44 It's 8:20. What's Mike doing? 77

> 44 He's eating breakfast. 77

DIGITAL
MORE
EXERCISES

DIGITAL
VIDEO
COACH

3 ▶3:44 **PRONUNCIATION** • *Intonation of questions* Use rising intonation for <u>yes</u> / <u>no</u> questions. Use falling intonation for information questions. Read and listen. Then listen again and repeat.

<u>Yes</u> /<u>no</u> questions	Information questions
1 Are you eating?	What are you eating?
2 Is he walking?	Where is he walking?
3 Are they watching a movie?	Who's watching a movie?
4 Is her family at home?	Where is her family?
5 Are you a teacher?	What do you do?

4 GRAMMAR • *The present participle: spelling rules*

base form		present participle	base form		present participle
talk	→	talking	make	→	making
read	→	reading	take	→	taking
watch	→	watching	come	→	coming

Remember:
shop → sho**pp**ing   get → ge**tt**ing   put → pu**tt**ing

GRAMMAR PRACTICE Write the present participle of each base form.

1 check ....   3 wash ....   5 drive ....

2 write ....   4 go ....   6 get up ....

▶3:45 **LISTENING COMPREHENSION** Listen. Complete each statement in the present continuous.

1 Sara's ....   4 Paul's ....

2 Dan's ....   5 Marla's ....

3 Eva's ....

NOW YOU CAN Ask about people's activities

▶3:46 **CONVERSATION MODEL** Read and listen.

A: Hello?
B: Hi, Grace. This is Jessica. What are you doing?
A: Well, actually, I'm doing the laundry right now.
B: Oh, I'm sorry. Should I call you back later?
A: Yes, thanks. Talk to you later. Bye.
B: Bye.

▶3:47 **RHYTHM AND INTONATION** Listen again and repeat.
Then practice the Conversation Model with a partner.

CONVERSATION ACTIVATOR With a partner, personalize the
conversation. Use your own names. Use the pictures or
use your own activities. Then change roles.

A: Hello?
B: Hi, ... This is .... What are you doing?
A: Well, actually, I .... right now.
B: Oh, I'm sorry. Should I call you back later?
A: Yes, thanks. Talk to you later. Bye.
B: ....

DON'T STOP!
Talk about a time to call back.
Call me at 3:00.
Call me tonight.

CHANGE PARTNERS Ask and talk about other activities.

EXTENSION

1 ▶3:48 READING Look at today's weather forecast.

December 16

	Seattle		Guadalajara		Toronto		Miami	
	High **7°C**	Low **2°C**	High **24°C**	Low **5°C**	High **-2°C**	Low **-3°C**	High **26°C**	Low **17°C**

Seattle
Morning: rainy
Afternoon: rainy
Evening: snowy / cold
Sunrise 7:52 A.M.
Sunset 4:18 P.M.

Guadalajara
Morning: sunny / warm
Afternoon: cloudy / warm
Evening: cool
Sunrise 7:23 A.M.
Sunset 6:16 P.M.

Toronto
Morning: cloudy / cold
Afternoon: mix of rain / snow
Evening: cold
Sunrise 7:45 A.M.
Sunset 4:42 P.M.

Miami
Morning: sunny / warm
Afternoon: sunny / hot
Evening: rainy / windy / cool
Sunrise 7:01 A.M.
Sunset 5:33 P.M.

2 READING COMPREHENSION Complete the chart for December 16ᵗʰ weather, according to the forecast in the Reading.

	in the morning	in the afternoon	in the evening
sunny	Guadalajara and Miami		
cloudy			
windy			
snowy			
rainy			
hot			
warm			
cold			
cool			

3 READING COMPREHENSION Look at the sunrise and sunset times. Answer the questions.

1 Which cities have sunrises before 7:30? ....

DIGITAL
MORE
EXERCISES

2 Which cities have sunsets before 5:00? ....

4 VOCABULARY / GRAMMAR GAME Team 1 mimes an activity. Team 2 asks questions. Use the activities from the box.

comb your hair	go to bed	check e-mail
drive	brush your teeth	listen to music
exercise	wash the dishes	put on makeup
talk on the phone	take out the garbage	
get dressed		
take a shower		
read		
watch TV		

Are you putting on makeup?

GRAMMAR BOOSTER
Unit 9 review • p. 141

PAIR WORK Create telephone conversations for Sam and Debbie on Thursday and on Saturday. Ask about activities and plans. Ask about the weather. For example:

This afternoon I'm going shopping. Then tonight I'm . . .

WRITING Write five <u>sentences about</u> your plans for this week. Use the present continuous. For example:

I'm going out for dinner on Saturday.

WRITING BOOSTER p. 148
Guidance for this writing exercise

Thursday, May 5, 1:20 P.M.

Saturday, May 7, 6:30 P.M.

NOW I CAN
- [ ] Describe today's weather.
- [ ] Discuss plans.
- [ ] Ask about people's activities.

COMMUNICATION GOALS

1 Discuss ingredients for a recipe.
2 Offer and ask for foods.
3 Invite someone to join you at the table.

UNIT 10 Food

LESSON 1 **GOAL** Discuss ingredients for a recipe

1 ▶4:02 **VOCABULARY** • *Foods: count nouns* Read and listen. Then listen again and repeat.

1 an egg

2 an onion

3 an apple

4 an orange

5 a lemon

6 a banana

7 a tomato

8 a potato

9 a pepper

10 beans

11 peas

VOCABULARY BOOSTER
More vegetables and fruits • p. 131

2 ▶4:03 **LISTENING COMPREHENSION** Listen to the conversations. Check the foods you hear in each conversation.

1		✓					✓	✓
2								
3								
4								
5								

3 **PAIR WORK** Which foods do you like? Tell your partner. Compare your likes and dislikes.

> 66 I don't like bananas, but I really like apples. 99

4 **GRAMMAR** • *How many / Are there any*

> **Use How many and Are there any with plural nouns.**
>
> **How many** onions **are there**? (Ten or twelve.)
> **How many** apples **are there** in the refrigerator? (I'm not sure. Maybe two.)
> **Are there any** lemons? (Yes, there are. OR Yes. There are three.)
> (No, there aren't. OR No. There aren't any.)

5 ▶4:04 VOCABULARY • *Places to keep food in a kitchen* Read and listen. Then listen again and repeat.

1 in the fridge (in the refrigerator) **2** on the shelf **3** on the counter

6 PAIR WORK Ask and answer questions about the Vocabulary pictures. Use <u>How many</u> and <u>Are there any</u>.

" How many potatoes are there on the shelf? "

" There are three. "

NOW YOU CAN Discuss ingredients for a recipe

▶4:05 CONVERSATION MODEL Read and listen.

A: How about some green bean salad?
B: Green bean salad? That sounds delicious! I love green beans.
A: Are there any beans in the fridge?
B: Yes, there are.
A: And do we have any onions?
B: I'm not sure. I'll check.

▶4:06 RHYTHM AND INTONATION Listen again and repeat.
Then practice the Conversation Model with a partner.

CONVERSATION ACTIVATOR With a partner, change the conversation. Use the recipes. Then change roles. Start like this:

A: How about some .... ?
B: ....? That sounds delicious! I love ....
A: Are there any .... ?
B: ....

Continue with the other ingredients in the recipe.

DON'T STOP!
Talk about what you need, want, have, and like.

 RECYCLE THIS LANGUAGE.

We need [onions].	And how about ___ ?
We don't have [eggs].	Uh-oh.
I really like [beans].	I don't know.
I don't like [peas].	Sounds nice.

CHANGE PARTNERS Discuss another recipe.

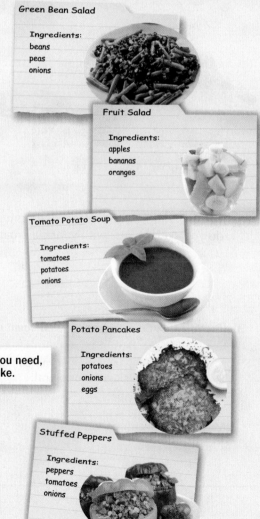

Green Bean Salad
Ingredients:
beans
peas
onions

Fruit Salad
Ingredients:
apples
bananas
oranges

Tomato Potato Soup
Ingredients:
tomatoes
potatoes
onions

Potato Pancakes
Ingredients:
potatoes
onions
eggs

Stuffed Peppers
Ingredients:
peppers
tomatoes
onions

1 ▶ 4:07 VOCABULARY • *Drinks and foods: non-count nouns* Read and listen. Then listen again and repeat.

DRINKS

1 water 2 coffee 3 tea 4 juice 5 milk 6 soda

FOODS

7 bread 8 pasta 9 rice 10 cheese 11 meat 12 chicken

13 fish 14 oil 15 butter 16 sugar 17 salt 18 pepper

2 VOCABULARY PRACTICE Which foods from the Vocabulary do you like? Discuss with your classmates.

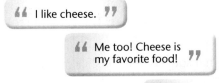

❝ I like cheese. ❞

❝ Me too! Cheese is my favorite food! ❞

❝ Not me. I really don't like cheese. ❞

3 GRAMMAR • *Count nouns and non-count nouns*

Count nouns name things you can count. They can be singular or plural.	Non-count nouns name things you cannot count. They are not singular or plural.
I want **an apple**. I like **bananas**. We have **three tomatoes** on the shelf.	I don't eat **sugar**. **Rice** is good for you. **Pasta** is my favorite food.

Be careful!

• **Use singular verbs with non-count nouns.**

Rice is good for you.
NOT Rice ~~are~~ good for you.

• **Don't use -s or a / an with non-count nouns.**

rice NOT ~~a rice~~
NOT ~~two rices~~

4 GRAMMAR PRACTICE Complete the chart. Be careful! Make your count nouns plural. But don't make your non-count nouns plural. Then compare with a partner.

I eat	pasta, peas . . .
I don't eat	
I drink	
I don't drink	

5 GRAMMAR • How much / Is there any

> **Use How much and Is there any to ask about non-count nouns.**
>
> **How much bread** does she want? (NOT ~~How many~~ bread does she want?)
> **How much milk** is there? (NOT ~~How many~~ milk is there?)
> **Is there any butter?** Yes, there is. / No, there isn't. OR No. There isn't any.

> **Remember:**
> Use How many with plural count nouns.
> **How many apples** are there?
> NOT ~~How much~~ apples are there?

6 ▶4:08 **VOCABULARY • Containers and quantities** Read and listen. Then listen again and repeat.

1 a box of pasta   2 a loaf of bread   3 a bottle of juice   4 a can of soda   5 a bag of onions

7 GRAMMAR PRACTICE Complete each question with How much or How many.

1 .... loaves of bread do you need?
2 .... bags of potatoes do we have?
3 .... cheese is there in the fridge?
4 .... sugar do you want in your tea?

5 .... eggs are there for the potato pancakes?
6 .... cans of tomatoes are there on the shelf?

NOW YOU CAN Offer and ask for foods

▶4:09 **CONVERSATION MODEL** Read and listen.

A: Would you like coffee or tea?
B: I'd like coffee, please. Thanks.
A: And would you like sugar?
B: No, thanks.
A: Please pass the butter.
B: Here you go.

▶4:10 **RHYTHM AND INTONATION** Listen again and repeat. Then practice the Conversation Model with a partner.

CONVERSATION ACTIVATOR With a partner, change the conversation. Use other foods and drinks. Then change roles.

A: Would you like .... or .... ?
B: I'd like ...., please. Thanks.
A: And would you like .... ?
B: ....
A: Please pass the ....
B: Here you go.

CHANGE PARTNERS Change the conversation again.

GOAL Invite someone to join you at the table

1 GRAMMAR • *The simple present tense and the present continuous*

> **Remember: Use the simple present tense with verbs <u>have</u>, <u>want</u>, <u>need</u>, and <u>like</u>.**
>
> I like coffee. NOT I'm liking coffee.
>
> **Use the simple present tense to describe habitual actions and with frequency adverbs.**
>
> I **cook** dinner every day.
> I never **eat** eggs for breakfast.

> **Use the present continuous for actions in progress right now.**
>
> We're **making** dinner now.
> She's **studying** English this year.

> **Be careful!**
> Don't say: We cook dinner now.
> Don't say: I am cooking dinner every day.

2 GRAMMAR PRACTICE Complete each statement or question with the simple present tense or the present continuous.

1 Who .... lunch in the kitchen right now?
   eat

2 Where .... he usually .... lunch—at home or at the office?
   eat

3 They .... a lot of sugar in their tea.
   not like

4 We .... the kitchen every day.
   clean

5 Elaine and Joe aren't here. They .... to work.
   drive

6 Why .... six cans of tomatoes?
   you / need
   .... tomato soup for lunch?
   you / make

7 .... to work tomorrow?
   she / go

8 How many boxes of rice .... ?
   he / want

9 I .... a bottle of juice in the fridge.
   not have

10 I can't talk right now. I ....
   study

3 GRAMMAR PRACTICE Look at Suzanne and her weekly schedule. Then write about Suzanne. What is she doing right now? What does she do at other times? Use the present continuous and the simple present tense.

May
10 Monday
Teach English [intermediate] at SCS: 10:00 A.M.

11 Tuesday
Work at home 8:00-12:00
Teach English [beginning] at Bank Street School: 4:00-6:00

12 Wednesday
Teach English [intermediate] at SCS: 10:00 A.M.

May
Thursday 13
Work at home 8:00-12:00
Teach English [beginning] at Bank Street School: 4:00-6:00

Friday 14
Study Chinese

Saturday 15
Laundry / shopping

Sunday 16
Cook for Mom and Dad

> *Suzanne is listening to music right now. She teaches English on Mondays, Tuesdays . . .*

4 PAIR WORK Ask and answer questions about Suzanne's activities. Use the simple present tense and the present continuous.

❝ Does Suzanne teach English? ❞

❝ Yes, she does. ❞

❝ What's Suzanne doing right now? ❞

❝ She's listening to music. ❞

5 ▶4:11 PRONUNCIATION • *Vowel sounds* Read and listen to the words in each group. Then listen again and repeat.

1 /i/	**2** /ɪ/	**3** /eɪ/	**4** /ɛ/	**5** /æ/
see	six	late	pepper	apple
tea	fish	potato	red	jacket
street	this	train	lemon	has

6 PAIR WORK Read aloud a word from the Pronunciation chart. Your partner says another word from the same group.

❝ fish ❞   ❝ six ❞

NOW YOU CAN Invite someone to join you at the table

1 ▶4:12 CONVERSATION MODEL Read and listen.

A: Hi, Alison. Nice to see you!
B: You too, Rita. Do you come here often?
A: Yes, I do. Would you like to join me?
B: Sure. What are you drinking?
A: Lemonade.
B: Mmm. Sounds good.

2 ▶4:13 RHYTHM AND INTONATION Listen again and repeat. Then practice the Conversation Model with a partner.

CONVERSATION ACTIVATOR With a partner, personalize the conversation. Use your own name and your own foods or drinks or use the pictures. Then change roles.

A: Hi, ... Nice to see you!
B: You, too, ... Do you come here often?
A: Yes, I do. Would you like to join me?
B: Sure. What are you .... ?
A: ....
B: Mmm. Sounds good.

DON'T STOP!
Offer foods and drinks.

 RECYCLE THIS LANGUAGE.
Would you like [coffee]?
Yes, thanks. / No, thanks.

CHANGE PARTNERS Invite another classmate to join you.

EXTENSION

1 ▶4:14 **READING** Read a recipe with only three ingredients.　　　　　▶4:15 **Cooking verbs**

Hungarian Cabbage and Noodles

Ingredients
1 large head of green cabbage
1/2 cup unsalted butter
11 ounces (700 grams) of
  egg noodles

1. Cut the cabbage into small slices.
2. Put the cabbage into a large bowl and add salt.
3. Put the cabbage into the refrigerator overnight.
4. The next day, drain the cabbage.
5. Melt the butter in a large pan.
6. Sauté the cabbage until it is light brown and very soft (30-40 minutes).
7. Cook the noodles and drain them. Mix them with the cabbage. Add lots of black pepper.

Source: Adapted from *Recipes 1-2-3* by Rozanne Gold (New York: Viking, 1997)

1 cut　2 add

3 put　4 drain

5 melt　6 sauté

7 cook

2 **READING COMPREHENSION** Answer the questions. Compare your answers with a partner.

1 How many ingredients does the recipe have? ....
2 What are the ingredients? ....
3 Is there any butter or oil in the recipe? ....

DIGITAL
MORE
EXERCISES

3 ▶4:16 **LISTENING COMPREHENSION** Listen to the radio cooking program. Write the correct quantity next to each ingredient. Then listen again and number the pictures in the correct order. Listen again and check your work.

Pasta with Garlic and Olive Oil

olive oil

Ingredients:
__ cloves of garlic
__ tablespoons of olive oil
__ box of pasta

tablespoon

cloves of garlic

1

4 **SPEAKING PRACTICE** Tell a partner what you eat for each meal.

❝ My favorite food for breakfast is eggs. ❞

GRAMMAR BOOSTER
Unit 10 review • p. 142

For additional language practice . . .

♫ **TOP NOTCH POP** • Lyrics p. 15
"Fruit Salad, Baby"

DIGITAL SONG　DIGITAL KARAOKE

DIGITAL GAMES

Monday /Wednesday / Friday
Michael: do laundry
(Monday only)
Sylvia: go shopping
Sylvia: cook dinner

Tuesday / Thursday / Saturday
Sylvia: take out the garbage
Michael: go shopping and cook
dinner

Sunday
No Chores!

Monday

MEMORY GAME Look at the pictures for one minute. Then close your books and say all the foods and drinks you remember. Use count and non-count nouns correctly.

DESCRIPTION Use the schedule and the pictures to describe Michael and Sylvia's activities and habitual actions. Use the present continuous and the simple present tense. For example:

> It's Tuesday. Michael is cooking dinner. Sylvia cooks dinner on Mondays.

PAIR WORK

1 Ask and answer questions about the pictures. Use <u>How many</u> and <u>How much</u>. Answer with <u>There is</u> and <u>There are</u>. For example:

> A: How many boxes of pasta are there on the counter?
> B: There are two.

2 Create conversations for Michael and Sylvia in the three pictures. For example:

> A: Would you like peas?
> B: Yes, please. And please pass the salt.

WRITING Write about what you eat on a typical day. Start like this:

> For breakfast I eat . . .

WRITING BOOSTER p. 148
Guidance for this writing exercise

Tuesday

Friday

NOW I CAN

☐ Discuss ingredients for a recipe.
☐ Offer and ask for foods.
☐ Invite someone to join me at the table.

COMMUNICATION GOALS
1 Tell someone about an event.
2 Describe your past activities.
3 Talk about your weekend.

UNIT 11 Past Events

GOAL Tell someone about an event

1 ▶4:19 VOCABULARY • *Describing times before today* Read and listen. Then listen again and repeat.

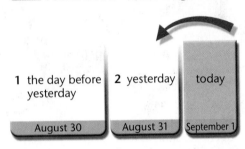

1 the day before yesterday   2 yesterday   today
August 30   August 31   September 1

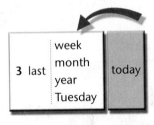

3 last | week / month / year / Tuesday | today

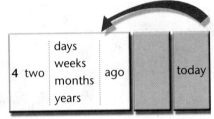

4 two | days / weeks / months / years | ago | today

▶4:20 **Years, decades, and centuries**

```
1900 = nineteen hundred
1901 = nineteen oh one
2000 = two thousand
2001 = two thousand one
2010 = twenty ten / two thousand ten
1990 to 1999 = the (nineteen) nineties
1901 to 2000 = the twentieth century
2001 to 2100 = the twenty-first century
```

2 ▶4:21 LISTENING COMPREHENSION Listen and circle the year.

1 1913 / 1930   3 1967 / 1976
2 2016 / 2060   4 2001 / 2021

3 PAIR WORK Choose five of the following years. Say a year to your partner. Your partner circles the year.

2008 1914 1910 1809 1955 1800

1998 1814 1615 2016 1922 2012

4 GRAMMAR • *The past tense of <u>be</u>: statements and questions; <u>there was</u> / <u>there were</u>*

Statements

Singular

| I He She | was wasn't | at school yesterday. |

There was a concert last night.

Plural

| We You They | were weren't | at home. |

There were two movies last weekend.

Contractions
was not → wasn't
were not → weren't

Questions

Singular
Was it cloudy yesterday?
  (Yes, it was. / No, it wasn't.)
Was there a game at the stadium?
  (Yes, there was. / No, there wasn't.)

Where was the party last night?
When was she in Italy?
Who was at the party?

Plural
Were you at the party last night?
  (Yes, we were. / No, we weren't.)
Were there students at the meeting?
  (Yes, there were. / No, there weren't.)

Where were they last weekend?
When were you at the bookstore?
Who were those students?"

5 GRAMMAR PRACTICE With a partner, take turns asking and answering the questions about the calendar. Today is April 20.

1 What day was yesterday?

> 66 Yesterday was April 19th. 99

2 What day was six days ago?

3 What day was one month ago?

4 What day was the day before yesterday?

5 What were the dates of last Saturday and Sunday?

6 What day was two months ago?

APRIL						
Sun	Mon	Tues	Wed	Thurs	Fri	Sat
	1	2	3	4	5	6
7	8	9	10	11	12	13
14	15	16	17	18	19	20
21	22	23	24	25	26	27
28	29	30				

6 ▶4:22 LISTENING COMPREHENSION Listen to the conversations about events. Then listen again and circle the correct day or month.

1 If today is Sunday, then the party was on (Saturday / Friday / Thursday).

2 If this is January, then their birthdays were in (February / December / January).

3 If today is Friday, then the game was on (Monday / Thursday / Wednesday).

NOW YOU CAN Tell someone about an event

▶4:23 CONVERSATION MODEL Read and listen.

A: Where were you last night?
B: What time?
A: At about 8:00.
B: I was at home. Why?
A: Because there was a great party at Celia's house.
B: There was? Too bad I wasn't there!

▶4:24 RHYTHM AND INTONATION Listen again and repeat. Then practice the Conversation Model with a partner.

CONVERSATION ACTIVATOR Make a list of places for an event in your city or town. Use the pictures for kinds of events. With a partner, change the conversation, using your events. Then change roles.

A: Where were you .... ?
B: What time?
A: At about ....
B: I was at .... Why?
A: Because there was a .... at ....
B: There was? Too bad I wasn't there!

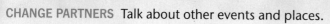

CHANGE PARTNERS Talk about other events and places.

LESSON **2** **GOAL** Describe your past activities

1 GRAMMAR • *The simple past tense: statements*

Use the past tense form for affirmative statements. Use <u>didn't</u> + the base form for negative statements.

Affirmative

| I
You
She | liked the movie. |
| We
They | |

Negative

| I
You
She | didn't like the concert. |
| We
They | |

Form: regular verbs
Add -<u>ed</u> to the base form.
If the base form ends in -<u>e</u>, add -<u>d</u>.

call → call**ed**   lik<u>e</u> → lik**ed**

BUT: study → stud**ied**
       shop → shop**ped**

Irregular verbs
Use the past tense form of irregular verbs in affirmative statements.
In negative statements, use <u>didn't</u> + the base form.

I **went** to a party. BUT I **didn't go** to the movies.
We **made** dinner. BUT We **didn't make** breakfast.

▶4:25 **Irregular verbs (Also see page 124.)**

buy	→	bought	eat	→	ate	read	→	read
come	→	came	get	→	got	say	→	said
cut	→	cut	go	→	went	see	→	saw
do	→	did	have	→	had	take	→	took
drink	→	drank	make	→	made	think	→	thought
drive	→	drove	put	→	put	write	→	wrote

2 ▶4:26 PRONUNCIATION • *The regular simple past tense ending* Listen. Then listen again and repeat.

1 /d/	**2** /t/	**3** /ɪd/
listened = listen/d/	liked = like/t/	wanted = want/ɪd/
exercised = exercise/d/	washed = wash/t/	needed = need/ɪd/

3 GRAMMAR PRACTICE Complete the e-mail. Use the simple past tense and the past tense of <u>be</u>.

< INBOX (12)   ∧ ∨

Hi, Lucille: Yesterday was a really nice day. I .... early, ... my teeth,
                                              1 get up   2 brush
.... breakfast, and .... my house—all before 8:30. Then I ....
   3 make   4 clean   5 work
until noon. After lunch, I .... to the weather report, and the weather ....
                          6 listen   7 be
warm. I .... all my grandchildren here. They .... here in the afternoon.
         8 invite   9 come
We .... together for a while, and then the younger children .... a nap.
   10 talk   11 take
The older ones .... to the park and .... soccer. At the end of the day, I
               12 go   13 play
.... dinner for all the children. They .... the dinner because it was pasta.
   14 cook   15 love
The kids .... everything and .... more! Great day!
         16 eat   17 want
Brian

90 UNIT 11

4 GRAMMAR • *The simple past tense: questions*

Question forms are the same with regular and irregular verbs.

Did	I you he she we they	watch TV last night? see a movie?	Yes, No,	I you he she we they	did. didn't.

Where **did** you **go** last weekend?
What time **did** they **go** out to dinner?
What **did** your friend **watch** on TV?
How many cups of coffee **did** she **drink**?
Who **did** they **see** yesterday?

Be careful!
Remember: Word order changes when Who is the subject of the sentence:
   Who **went** to the mall this morning? (We did.)

5 GRAMMAR PRACTICE Complete the conversations, using the simple past tense.

1 A: Where .... on Saturday?
          ‹1 your family / go›
   B: .... to the movies. .... a
          ‹2 We / go›   ‹3 we / see›
   good family movie.

   A: .... out to eat afterwards?
          ‹4 you / go›
   B: Yes, we ....
                       ‹5›   ‹6 We / eat›
   Indonesian food. .... a lot of pepper.
                           ‹7 It / have›
   A: But ....
          ‹8 I / think›   ‹9 your husband / not like›
   peppery food.

   B: Actually, ... a little and
                     ‹10 he / eat›
   .... it was good.
   ‹11 he / say›

2 A: .... out the garbage this morning?
          ‹12 who / take›
   B: Actually, Laura ....
                               ‹13›
   A: And .... the laundry?
              ‹14 who / do›
   B: I'm not sure. But I think .... the
                                      ‹15 Laura / do›
   laundry this morning, too.

   A: That's great, but .... any household
                               ‹16 you / do›
   chores?

   B: Me? Last week .... all the chores:
                          ‹17 I / do›
   .... shopping, and .... home
   ‹18 I / go›   ‹19 I / come›
   early, and .... dinner every night.
                ‹20 I / make›

NOW YOU CAN Describe your past activities

▶4:27 **CONVERSATION MODEL** Read and listen.

A: So what did you do yesterday?
B: Well, I got up at seven, I made breakfast, and then I went to work.
A: What about after work? Did you do anything special?
B: Not really. I just made dinner and watched a movie.

▶4:28 **RHYTHM AND INTONATION** Listen again and repeat.
Then practice the Conversation Model with a partner.

CONVERSATION ACTIVATOR With a partner, personalize
the conversation. Describe your past activities. Then
change roles.

A: So what did you do .... ?
B: Well, I ...., and then I ....
A: What about .... ? Did you do anything special?
B: ....

CHANGE PARTNERS Ask about other past activities.

DON'T STOP!
Ask more questions.
   Did you [wash the dishes]?
   Who [took out the garbage]?
   When did you [go to the movies]?

Ideas
• household chores
• leisure activities
• entertainment events

GOAL Talk about your weekend

VOCABULARY BOOSTE

More outdoor activities • p.

DIGITAL FLASH CARDS

1 ▶ 4:29 **VOCABULARY** • *Outdoor activities* Read and listen. Then listen again and repeat.

1 go to the beach

2 go running

3 go bike riding

4 go for a walk

5 go swimming

6 go for a drive

2 **PAIR WORK** Ask and answer questions with <u>When</u> and <u>How often</u> and the Vocabulary. Use the simple present tense.

❝ How often do you go to the beach? ❞

❝ I go about once a month. ❞

3 ▶ 4:30 **LISTENING COMPREHENSION** Listen to the conversations. Then check the correct picture to complete each statement.

1 Rosalie went ___.

a

b

2 She's going ___.

a

b

3 They're going ___.

a

b

4 He went ___.

a

b

Talk about your weekend

1 ▶4:31 **CONVERSATION MODEL** Read and listen.

A: Did you have a good weekend?
B: Let me think. . . . Oh, yeah. I had a great weekend.
A: What did you do?
B: Well, on Saturday, my friends and I went bike riding and to a movie. Then on Sunday, I went for a drive. What about you?
A: Well, on Saturday, the weather was great, so I went for a walk. And on Sunday, my family and I went to the beach.

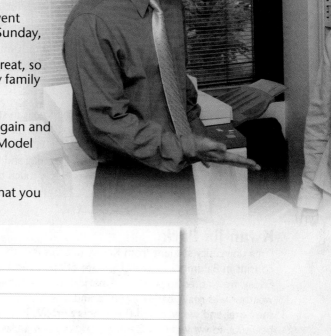

▶4:32 **RHYTHM AND INTONATION** Listen again and repeat. Then practice the Conversation Model with a partner.

NOTEPADDING On the notepad, write what you did on the weekend.

On Saturday
On Sunday

CONVERSATION ACTIVATOR With a partner, personalize the conversation. Use your own information and the simple past tense.

A: Did you have a good weekend?
B: Let me think . . . Oh, yeah. I ....
A: What did you do?
B: Well, ... Then .... What about you?
A: Well, on .... , the weather was .... , so I .... And on Sunday, ...

CHANGE PARTNERS Talk about more weekend activities.

DON'T STOP!

Ask your partner more questions.

 RECYCLE THIS LANGUAGE.

Really?
Did you do anything special?
What time did you come home?
Is [the beach] far from here?
Do you [go swimming] often?
How often do you [go bike riding]?

1 ▶ 4:33 READING Read about what people did last weekend.

fz FriendsZone 🔍

What did you do last weekend?

Gaby Pérez   Location: Mexico

My husband and I live in Guadalajara, in the Mexican state of Jalisco. We love the beach, so last Friday we got up early and drove to Puerto Vallarta, about three and a half hours from home. The drive was nice, and we sang as we drove. On Friday night we had a great dinner at a wonderful fish restaurant. Then we got up early on Saturday, and because the weather was great, we went to the beach before breakfast! Sunday was pretty much the same. What a great weekend!

Comment [   ]

Kwan-Jin Park   Location: Korea

I'm a university student from Korea, but this month I'm visiting my aunt and uncle and my cousins in Baltimore, in the U.S. state of Maryland. Last weekend, we went to New York. On Friday, we wanted to go to an American restaurant and then to an outdoor concert. But the weather was really bad—it rained, and it was so cold! We didn't go to the concert. We ate in the hotel, and we watched the concert on TV! But on Saturday and Sunday, the weather was beautiful, so we went to Central Park and saw a play outdoors. We ate right there in the park, and we had a great, great time. I loved New York.

Comment [   ]

Paul Martin   Location: Canada

Last weekend was actually pretty nice. I live in Montreal, in the Canadian province of Quebec. I invited my friends here, and we went for a walk in the Old City. We ate delicious food at a great restaurant. On Saturday, my girlfriend came here from Quebec City. We went dancing, and we stayed out so late. Here's a great picture. On Sunday, we went to the movies and to the mall. We bought new clothes. Montreal has some wonderful stores.

Comment [   ]

2 READING COMPREHENSION Write one yes / no question and one information question about Gaby, Kwan-Jin, and Paul. Then answer a partner's questions.

	Yes / no questions	Information questions
Gaby		
Kwan-Jin		
Paul		

Ideas
Was [Gaby] in . . .
Did [Kwan-Jin] . . .
Where was ___ . . .   last weekend?
Where did ___ . . .   last Sunday?
What did ___ . . .   on Saturday?
Who was with ___ . . .   on Friday night
When did ___ . . .
What did ___ . . .

DIGITAL
MORE
EXERCISES

3 SPEAKING / GRAMMAR PRACTICE Ask your partner questions about an activity in the past. Then tell your classmates about the activity. Use past-time expressions.

For additional language practice . . .

GRAMMAR BOOSTER
Unit 11 review • p. 143

🎵 TOP NOTCH POP • Lyrics p. 1
"My Favorite Day"

DIGITAL SONG   DIGITAL KARAOKE

VERB GAME Form two teams. Look at the pictures for one minute. Then close your books. Each team makes a list of all the actions in the pictures. The team with the most actions wins. For example:

watch TV   do the laundry

STORY Tell a story about one of the people. Use past-time expressions. For example:

Last weekend, Karen went to a concert with her friends. She ...

PAIR WORK With a partner, play the role of Don or Karen. Discuss your activities from the day before and the weekend before. Start like this:

So what did you do [last weekend] ...?

WRITING Choose one of the following topics:
Write about Don and Karen. Write about what they did.
Write about your weekend. Write about what you did.

For example:

Last weekend I went to the beach ...

WRITING BOOSTER p. 149
Guidance for this writing exercise

Yesterday

Yesterday

Last Weekend

Saturday

Last Weekend

Saturday

Sunday

Sunday

NOW I CAN

☐ Tell someone about an event.
☐ Describe my past activities.
☐ Talk about my weekend.

COMMUNICATION GOALS
1 Describe appearance.
2 Show concern about an injury.
3 Suggest a remedy.

LESSON 1 **GOAL** Describe appearance

DIGITAL FLASH CARDS

1 ▶4:36 **VOCABULARY** • *Adjectives to describe hair* Read and listen. Then listen again and repeat.

1 black **2** brown **3** red **4** blonde **5** gray **6** white

7 dark **8** light

14 He's **bald.**
15 He has a **mustache.**
16 He has a **beard.**
17 He wears **glasses.**

9 straight **10** wavy **11** curly **12** long **13** short

DIGITAL FLASH CARDS

2 ▶4:37 **VOCABULARY** • *The face* Read and listen. Then listen again and repeat.

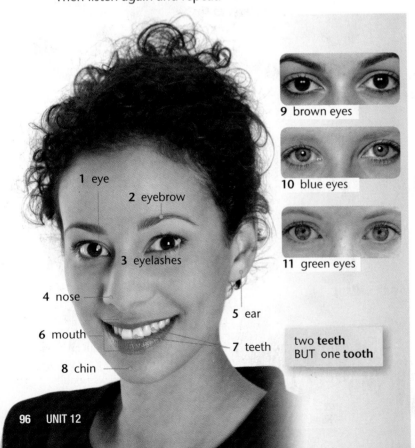

1 eye
2 eyebrow
3 eyelashes
4 nose
5 ear
6 mouth
7 teeth
8 chin

9 brown eyes
10 blue eyes
11 green eyes

two **teeth** BUT one **tooth**

3 ▶4:38 **LISTENING COMPREHENSION** Listen to the descriptions. Write the number of the conversation in the circle.

With <u>be</u>	With <u>have</u>
Her **eyes** are **blue**.	She has **blue** eyes.
Their **hair** is **gray**.	They have **gray** hair.
Her **eyelashes** are **long and dark**.	She has **long, dark** eyelashes.

> **Remember:**
> **Adjectives come before the nouns they describe.**
> She has blue eyes. NOT She has ~~eyes blue~~.
> **Adjectives are never plural.**
> She has blue eyes. NOT She has ~~blues~~ eyes.
> Her eyes are blue. NOT Her eyes are ~~blues~~.

5 GRAMMAR PRACTICE Complete each sentence with the correct form of <u>be</u> or <u>have</u>.

1 A: What does your brother look like?

B: Well, he .... a mustache and wavy hair. And he wears glasses.

2 A: What does your mother look like?

B: Her hair .... curly and black.

3 A: What does her father look like?

B: He .... a short, gray beard.

4 A: What does his grandmother look like?

B: She .... curly, gray hair and beautiful eyes.

5 A: What does his sister look like?

B: His sister? Her hair .... long and pretty!

6 A: What do your brothers look like?

B: They .... straight, black hair, and they wear glasses.

NOW YOU CAN Describe appearance

▶4:39 **CONVERSATION MODEL** Read and listen.

A: Who's that? She looks familiar.

B: Who?

A: The woman with the long, dark hair.

B: Oh, that's Ivete Sangalo. She's a singer from Brazil.

A: No kidding!

▶4:40 **RHYTHM AND INTONATION** Listen again and repeat. Then practice the Conversation Model with a partner.

CONVERSATION ACTIVATOR With a partner, change the conversation. Talk about the people in the photos. (OR use your own photos.) Then change roles.

A: Who's that? .... looks familiar.

B: Who?

A: The .... with the ....

B: Oh, that's .... 's .... from ....

A: No kidding!

DON'T STOP!
Say more about the person's appearance.

🔄 **RECYCLE THIS LANGUAGE.**

He's so [good-looking / handsome / old].
She's very [pretty / young / tall].
Her hair is so [wavy / pretty / short].
His eyes are very [blue / dark].

CHANGE PARTNERS Talk about other people.

Ivete Sangalo
singer (Brazil)

Andrea Bocelli
singer (Italy)

Amy Adams
actor (U.S.)

Emeli Sandé
singer (U.K.)

Chris Hemsworth
actor (Australia)

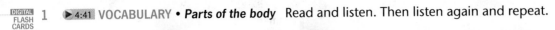

LESSON 2 — GOAL: Show concern about an injury

1 ▶ 4:41 **VOCABULARY • *Parts of the body*** Read and listen. Then listen again and repeat.

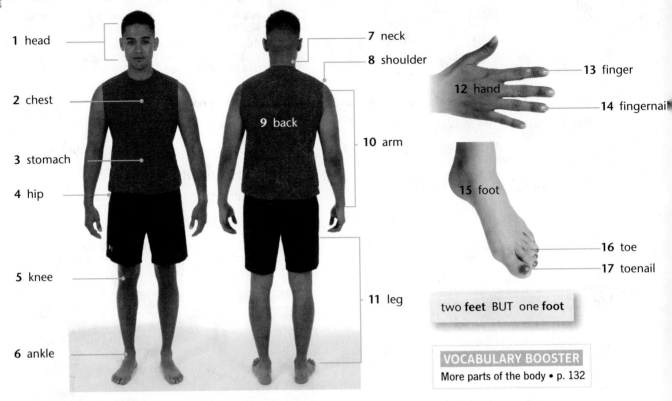

1 head
2 chest
3 stomach
4 hip
5 knee
6 ankle

7 neck
8 shoulder
9 back
10 arm
11 leg

12 hand
13 finger
14 fingernail
15 foot
16 toe
17 toenail

two **feet** BUT one **foot**

VOCABULARY BOOSTER
More parts of the body • p. 132

2 **GAME / VOCABULARY PRACTICE** Follow a classmate's directions. If you make a mistake, sit down.

Touch your toes.

▶ 4:43 base form	past form
burn →	**burned**
hurt →	**hurt**
cut →	**cut**
break →	**broke**
fall →	**fell**

3 ▶ 4:42 **VOCABULARY • *Accidents and injuries*** Read and listen. Then listen again and repeat.

1 He **burned** his finger.
2 She **hurt** her back.
3 She **cut** her hand.
4 He **broke** his arm.
5 He **fell** down.

98 UNIT 12

4 ▶4:44 **LISTENING COMPREHENSION** Listen to the conversations. Write each injury. Then listen again and check your work.

1 She ...*burned her arm*........ .   **4** He ....

2 He ....   **5** She ....

3 She ....   **6** He ....

5 ▶4:45 **PRONUNCIATION** • *More vowel sounds* Read and listen. Then listen again and repeat. Then practice saying the words on your own.

1 /u/	**2** /ʊ/	**3** /oʊ/	**4** /ɔ/	**5** /ɑ/
tooth	should	nose	awful	blonde
blue	good	toe	fall	hot
food	foot	broke	long	wash

NOW YOU CAN **Show concern about an injury**

▶4:46 **CONVERSATION MODEL** Read and listen.

A: Hey, Evan. What happened?
B: I broke my ankle.
A: I'm sorry to hear that. Does it hurt a lot?
B: Actually, no. It doesn't.

▶4:48
Ways to express concern
I'm sorry to hear that.
Oh, no.
That's too bad.

▶4:47 **RHYTHM AND INTONATION** Listen again and repeat. Then practice the Conversation Model with a partner.

CONVERSATION ACTIVATOR With a partner, change the conversation. Use the pictures for ideas. Then change roles.

A: Hey, ... What happened?
B: I ....
A: .... Does it hurt a lot?
B: Actually, ... It ....

CHANGE PARTNERS Discuss other injuries.

1 ▶4:49 VOCABULARY • *Ailments* Read and listen. Then listen again and repeat.

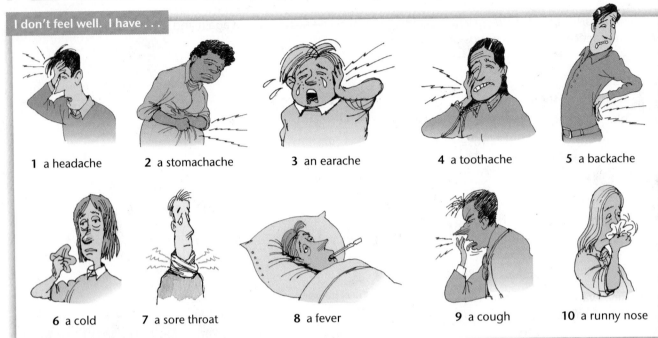

I don't feel well. I have . . .

1 a headache **2** a stomachache **3** an earache **4** a toothache **5** a backache

6 a cold **7** a sore throat **8** a fever **9** a cough **10** a runny nose

2 VOCABULARY PRACTICE Tell your partner about a time you had an ailment. Use the Vocabulary.

" I had a headache last week. "

" Really? I never have headaches. "

3 ▶4:50 VOCABULARY • *Remedies* Read and listen. Then listen again and repeat.

   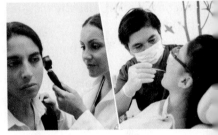

1 take something **2** lie down **3** have some tea **4** see a doctor / see a dentist

4 GRAMMAR • *Should + base form for suggestions*

Use should with the base form of a verb.

| I
You
He
She
We
They | should take something.
shouldn't go to work. |

You **should see** a doctor.

He **shouldn't go** to school today.

5 ▶4:51 **LISTENING COMPREHENSION** Listen to the conversations. Check the correct ailments. Then complete the suggestion for a remedy each person gives. Use should.

	a cold	a fever	a headache	a stomachache	a sore throat	a backache	a toothache	Remedy
1	☐	☐	☐	☐	☐	☐	☐	She *should take something.*
2	☐	☐	☐	☐	☐	☐	☐	He
3	☐	☐	☐	☐	☐	☐	☐	She
4	☐	☐	☐	☐	☐	☐	☐	He
5	☐	☐	☐	☐	☐	☐	☐	She
6	☐	☐	☐	☐	☐	☐	☐	He

6 **VOCABULARY / GRAMMAR PRACTICE** Work with a partner. Listen to your partner's ailments. Suggest remedies. Use should or shouldn't.

Partner A's ailments

1 I have a backache.

2 I don't feel well. I think I have a fever.

3 My son doesn't feel well. He has a cough.

Partner B's ailments

1 I have a bad toothache.

2 I have a sore throat.

3 My wife feels really bad. She has a stomachache.

NOW YOU CAN Suggest a remedy

▶4:52 **CONVERSATION MODEL** Read and listen.

A: I don't feel well.
B: What's wrong?
A: I have a headache.
B: Oh, that's too bad. You really should take something.
A: Good idea. Thanks.
B: I hope you feel better.

▶4:54
Ways to say you're sick
I don't feel well.
I feel terrible.
I don't feel so good.

▶4:53 **RHYTHM AND INTONATION** Listen again and repeat. Then practice the Conversation Model with a partner.

CONVERSATION ACTIVATOR With a partner, change the conversation. Suggest a remedy with should. Then change roles.

A: ....
B: What's wrong?
A: ....
B: .... You really ....
A: .... Thanks.
B: I hope you feel better.

DON'T STOP!
Give other advice, using should or shouldn't.
Ideas
✓ go to bed   ✗ go to class
✓ take a nap   ✗ exercise

CHANGE PARTNERS Discuss other ailments.

EXTENSION

1 ▶4:55 **READING** Look at the photos and read the descriptions. Do you know these famous people?

Johnny Depp

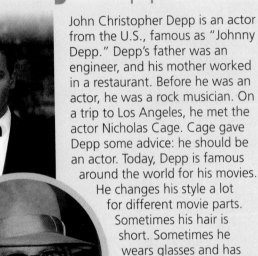

John Christopher Depp is an actor from the U.S., famous as "Johnny Depp." Depp's father was an engineer, and his mother worked in a restaurant. Before he was an actor, he was a rock musician. On a trip to Los Angeles, he met the actor Nicholas Cage. Cage gave Depp some advice: he should be an actor. Today, Depp is famous around the world for his movies. He changes his style a lot for different movie parts. Sometimes his hair is short. Sometimes he wears glasses and has long hair. And sometimes he doesn't shave and has a mustache and a beard. Many people think he is very handsome—and a very good actor. Depp has two children, Lily-Rose and Jack.

Shakira

Shakira Isabel Mebarak Ripoll is a singer and songwriter from Barranquilla, Colombia. Her father's family came from Lebanon, so she often listened and danced to traditional Arab music. In 1996 Shakira's Spanish-language album Pies Descalzos made her famous all over Latin America and Spain, and she became a star. In 200 she recorded her first songs in English on the album Laundry Service. Today, Shakira is a TV star too, and she is famous all over the world. When Shakira was young, she had long black hair. Late she changed her hair styl to long and blonde. But he fans think she is beautiful in any style.

2 **READING COMPREHENSION** Answer the questions. Write the person.

| Johnny Depp | Depp's father | Shakira | Nicholas Cage |
| Depp's children | Depp's mother | Shakira's grandparents | |

1 Who acts in movies? ....
2 Who is a grandmother? ....
3 Who is from Lebanon? ....
4 Whose father was a musician? ....
5 Who gave good advice? ....
6 Who was an engineer? ....

3 **PAIR WORK** Partner A describes Shakira in her two pictures. Partner B describes Johnny Depp in his two pictures. Which pictures do you like?

> ❝ I like Shakira in the first picture. She has... ❞

4 **DISCUSSION** What kind of hair is good-looking for women? What kind of hair is good-looking for me

> ❝ I like short, wavy hair on men. ❞

DIGITAL
MORE
EXERCISES

5 **GROUP WORK** Describe someone in your class. Your classmates guess who it is.

> ❝ She's short and very good-looking. She has long hair and brown eyes. She's wearing a white blouse and a blue skirt. ❞

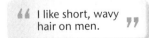

GRAMMAR BOOSTE
Unit 12 review • p. 143

GAME Play in groups of three. Partner A: Describe a person's ailment or injury. Partners B and C: Who can point to the picture first?
For example: *He has a headache.*

PAIR WORK

1 Describe a person. Your partner points to the picture. For example: *He has brown hair.*

2 Suggest a remedy. Your partner points to the picture. For example: *She should see a doctor.*

3 Create a conversation for each situation. Start like this: *What happened?* OR *I feel terrible.*

WRITING Describe someone you know. Use the vocabulary from this unit and from Unit 4. For example:

> My friend Sam is very handsome.
> He has short, curly hair . . .

WRITING BOOSTER p. 149
Guidance for this writing exercise

✓ NOW I CAN

☐ Describe appearance.
☐ Show concern about an injury.
☐ Suggest a remedy.

UNIT 13 Abilities and Requests

COMMUNICATION GOALS
1 Discuss your abilities.
2 Politely decline an invitation.
3 Ask for and agree to do a favor.

LESSON 1 **GOAL** Discuss your abilities

VOCABULARY BOOSTER
More musical instruments • p. 133

DIGITAL FLASH CARDS

1 ▶5:02 VOCABULARY • *Abilities* Read and listen. Then listen again and repeat.

1 sing

2 dance

3 swim

4 play the guitar / the violin

5 ski

6 cook

7 sew

8 knit

9 draw

10 paint

11 drive

12 fix things

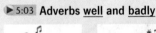
▶5:03 **Adverbs well and badly**

Tom sings well.   Ryan sings badly.

2 **VOCABULARY PRACTICE** Write three things you do well and three things you do badly.

1 I sing well.	**1** I dance badly.
1	1
2	2
3	3

3 **PAIR WORK** Tell your partner about your abilities. Use your sentences from Vocabulary Practice with <u>and</u> and <u>but</u>.

❝ I sing well, **but** I dance badly. ❞

❝ I draw well, **and** I paint well, too. ❞

4 **GROUP WORK** Tell your class about some of your partner's abilities.

❝ Ann sings well, **but** she dances badly. She plays the guitar, **and** she plays the violin, too. ❞

To talk about ability, use <u>can</u> or <u>can't</u> and the base form of a verb.

Carrie **can** play the guitar.

Josie **can't** cook.

Questions
Can you **play** the guitar?
Can he **speak** English?

Short answers
Yes, I **can**. / No, I **can't**.
Yes, he **can**. / No, he **can't**.

Use <u>can</u> or <u>can't</u> with <u>well</u> to indicate degree of ability.
She **can** play the guitar, but she **can't** play **well**.

can't = can not = cannot

GRAMMAR PRACTICE Complete each conversation with <u>can</u> or <u>can't</u> and the base form of a verb.

1 A: .... you .... the guitar?
B: Yes, I .... But I don't play well.

2 A: .... Gwen .... well?
B: Yes, she .... She swims very well.

3 A: .... your brother .... ?
B: My brother? No. He .... cook at all.

4 A: .... Gloria .... English well?
B: No, she .... She needs this class.

5 A: .... your mother .... ?
B: Yes. She knits very well.

6 A: .... your sisters .... ?
B: Yes. They go skiing every weekend.

NOW YOU CAN Discuss your abilities

▶5:04 **CONVERSATION MODEL** Read and listen.

A: Can you draw?
B: Actually, yes, I can. Can you?
A: No, I can't.
B: Really? That's too bad.

▶5:06 **Ways to respond**
A: I can draw. | **A:** I can't draw.
B: That's great! | **B:** That's too bad.

▶5:05 **RHYTHM AND INTONATION** Listen again and repeat. Then practice the Conversation Model with a partner.

CONVERSATION ACTIVATOR With a partner, personalize the conversation. Discuss your abilities. Then change roles.

A: Can you ....?
B: Actually, ..., I .... Can you?
A: ...., I ....
B: Really? That's ....

DON'T STOP!
Ask more questions. Say more about your abilities.

4 **CHANGE PARTNERS** Discuss other abilities.

RECYCLE THIS LANGUAGE.

What do you [draw]?	I draw [people].
How often do you [ski]?	I ski [every weekend].
Where do you [sing]?	I sing [in the shower].

1 ▶ 5:07 VOCABULARY • *Reasons for not doing something* Read and listen. Then listen again and repeat.

1 She's busy.

2 They're not hungry.

3 She's full.

4 He's tired.

5 It's early.

6 It's late.

2 PAIR WORK Tell your partner about a time you were busy, tired, or full.

> " Last week, I worked late every day. I was so tired. "

3 GRAMMAR • *Too* + *adjective*

> **Too** makes an adjective stronger. It usually gives it a negative meaning.
>
> I'm **too busy**. I can't talk right now.
> I'm **too tired**. Let's not go to the movies.
> It's **too late**. I should go to bed.

> **Be careful!**
> **Don't use <u>too</u> with a positive adjective.**
> She's so pretty!
> NOT She's ~~too pretty~~!

4 GRAMMAR PRACTICE Complete each sentence. Use <u>too</u> and an adjective.

1 I don't want these shoes. They're ....

2 It's .... today. She can't go swimming.

3 I'm .... I can't read right now.

4 He doesn't want that shirt. It's ....

5 I can't talk right now. I'm ....

6 It's .... for a movie. We should go to bed.

1 ▶5:08 **CONVERSATION MODEL** Read and listen.

A: Hey, Sue. Let's go to a movie.
B: I'm really sorry, Paul, but I'm too busy.
A: That's OK. Maybe some other time.

2 ▶5:09 **RHYTHM AND INTONATION** Listen again and repeat. Then practice the Conversation Model with a partner.

3 **CONVERSATION ACTIVATOR** With a partner, change the conversation. Suggest a different activity. Use the Vocabulary and the photos (or your own ideas). Then change roles.

A: Hey, ... Let's go ....
B: I'm really sorry, ..., but ....
A: That's OK. Maybe some other time.

DON'T STOP!
Suggest another day or time.

RECYCLE THIS LANGUAGE.
How about [tomorrow / this weekend / this evening / at 6:00]?
Sounds great! / OK!
I'm not hungry.
I'm too [tired / busy / full].
It's too [early / late].
It's too [windy / hot / cold / rainy] today.

CHANGE PARTNERS Suggest other activities and give other reasons.

LESSON 3 | **GOAL** Ask for and agree to do a favor

1 GRAMMAR • *Polite requests with Could you + base form*

> Use **Could you** and the base form of a verb to make a request.
> **Could you wash** the dishes?
>
> Use **please** to make a request more polite.
> **Could you please** wash the dishes?

2 ▶5:10 VOCABULARY • *Favors* Read and listen. Then listen again and repeat.

1 Could you please **help me**?

2 Could you please **open** the window?
Also: open the door / refrigerator

3 Could you please **close** the door?
Also: close the window / microwave

4 Could you please **turn on** the light?
Also: turn on the stove /computer

5 Could you please **turn off** the TV?
Also: turn off the microwave / light

6 Could you please **hand me** my glasses?
Also: hand me my sweater / book

3 VOCABULARY / GRAMMAR PRACTICE Complete the polite requests. Use <u>Could you please</u>. Use the Vocabulary and other verbs you know.

1 It's a little hot in here. *Could you please open* .... the window?

2 I have a headache. .... the TV?

3 .... my jacket? I'm going for a walk.

4 I'm going to bed. .... the computer?

5 I want to read a book. .... my glasses?

6 .... shopping? We need milk.

7 I'm busy right now. .... the garbage?

8 Let's watch a movie. .... the TV?

▶5:11 **LISTENING COMPREHENSION** Listen to the conversations. Then complete each request.

1 Could you ....close the window.., please?

2 Could you ....?

3 Could you please ....?

4 Could you please ....?

5 Could you ....?

5 ▶5:12 **PRONUNCIATION** • *Blending of sounds: Could you* . . . Read and listen. Then listen again and repeat.

/ˈkʊdʒu/

1 **Could you** please open the window?

2 **Could you** please close the door?

6 **VOCABULARY / PRONUNCIATION PRACTICE** Look again at the Vocabulary. With a partner, take turns reading the requests aloud. Pay attention to blending of sounds in Could you.

NOW YOU CAN Ask for and agree to do a favor

▶5:13 **CONVERSATION MODEL** Read and listen.

A: Could you do me a favor?
B: Of course.
A: It's very cold. Could you please close the window?
B: Sure. No problem.

▶5:15 **Ways to agree to a request**
Sure.
No problem.
Of course.
My pleasure.
OK.

▶5:14 **RHYTHM AND INTONATION** Listen again and repeat. Then practice the Conversation Model with a partner.

CONVERSATION ACTIVATOR With a partner, change the conversation. Ask for a different favor. Then change roles.

A: Could you do me a favor?
B: ....
A: .... Could you please .... ?
B: ....

DON'T STOP!
Ask for more favors:
Could you please ___, too?

RECYCLE THIS LANGUAGE.
It's very [hot / windy].   I'm so [tired / hungry].
I'm making lunch.   I'm very busy right now.
I'm going to bed.

CHANGE PARTNERS Ask for other favors.

Ideas for favors

turn on the ___	help me
turn off the ___	do the laundry
open the ___	make dinner
close the ___	take out the garbage
hand me my ___	wash the dishes
	clean the house

EXTENSION

1 ▶ 5:16 READING Read the article.

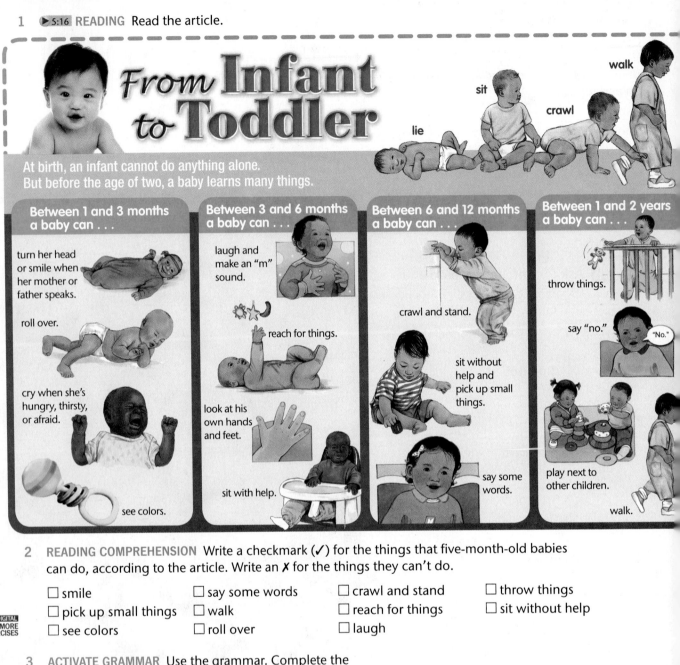

From Infant to Toddler

At birth, an infant cannot do anything alone.
But before the age of two, a baby learns many things.

lie   sit   crawl   walk

Between 1 and 3 months a baby can . . .

turn her head or smile when her mother or father speaks.

roll over.

cry when she's hungry, thirsty, or afraid.

see colors.

Between 3 and 6 months a baby can . . .

laugh and make an "m" sound.

reach for things.

look at his own hands and feet.

sit with help.

Between 6 and 12 months a baby can . . .

crawl and stand.

sit without help and pick up small things.

say some words.

Between 1 and 2 years a baby can . . .

throw things.

say "no."

play next to other children.

walk.

2 READING COMPREHENSION Write a checkmark (✓) for the things that five-month-old babies can do, according to the article. Write an ✗ for the things they can't do.

☐ smile ☐ say some words ☐ crawl and stand ☐ throw things
☐ pick up small things ☐ walk ☐ reach for things ☐ sit without help
☐ see colors ☐ roll over ☐ laugh

DIGITAL
MORE
EXERCISES

3 ACTIVATE GRAMMAR Use the grammar. Complete the sentences about what a baby cannot do.

At one month, *a baby can't crawl.*

1 At two months,
2 At five months,
3 At eleven months,
4 At sixteen months,

GRAMMAR BOOSTER
Unit 13 review • p. 144

For additional language practice . . .

4 GROUP WORK Discuss things children can and can't do at other ages.

❝ At three, a child can't ride a bicycle. But at eight, a child can do some household chores. ❞

🎵 TOP NOTCH POP • Lyrics p. 15
"She Can't Play Guitar"

DIGITAL SONG   DIGITAL KARAOKE

PAIR WORK

1 Create conversations for the people.

A: Let's ___.   B: I'm really sorry, but...

2 Ask and answer questions with <u>Can</u> about the people in Apartments 2A and 2B. For example:

Can she ___? / Can he ___?

GAME Make true and false statements about the picture. For example:

A: The girl in Apartment 2A is opening the window.

B: That's false. She's closing the window.

STORY Create a story about what is happening in the apartment building. Start like this:

It's 9:30. In Apartment 2B, a boy is playing the violin . . .

WRITING Describe some things people can and can't do when they are 80 years old. For example:

At eighty, some people can't drive, but my grandfather can.

WRITING BOOSTER p. 149
Guidance for this writing exercise

Apartment 3A

Could you please ___?

Apartment 2A

Apartment 2B

Could you please ___?

✔ NOW I CAN

☐ Discuss my abilities.
☐ Politely decline an invitation.
☐ Ask for and agree to do a favor.

Apartment 1A

Let's ___.

LESSON 1 **GOAL** Get to know someone's life story

1 ▶5:19 **VOCABULARY** • *Some life events* Read and listen. Then listen again and repeat.

1 be born

2 grow up

3 go to school

4 move

5 study

6 graduate

2 ▶5:20 **PRONUNCIATION** • *Diphthongs*
Listen and repeat.

1 /aɪ/	**2** /aʊ/	**3** /ɔɪ/
my	how	boy
I	noun	oil
tie	town	boil

3 **PRONUNCIATION PRACTICE** Look at the Vocabulary pictures. Ask and answer the questions out loud with a partner. Use the correct pronunciation of the diphthongs.
1 What's the boy's first name?
2 What's his last name?
3 What school did he go to?
4 What university did he graduate from?

4 ▶5:21 **LISTENING COMPREHENSION** Listen to the conversation about Graciela Boyd's life story. Which statement about Graciela's life is true?

☐ She was born in Boston and lives there now.

☐ She was born in London and lives in Boston now.

☐ She was born in Costa Rica and lives in Boston now.

5 ▶5:22 Listen again. Circle the correct word or words to complete each statement. If necessary, listen again.

1 Graciela's mother is from (Costa Rica / Boston).
2 Graciela was born in (Costa Rica / London).
3 Her father is (American / British).

4 Graciela's mother is a/an (Spanish / English) teacher.
5 Graciela grew up in (London / Boston).
6 In May, Graciela is graduating from (the university / medical school).

6 **PAIR WORK** Use the questions to interview your partner. Then tell the class about your partner.
1 When and where were you born? What about other people in your family?
2 Where did you grow up? What about other people in your family?

7 ►5:23 VOCABULARY • *Academic subjects* Read and listen. Then listen again and repeat.

VOCABULARY BOOSTER
More academic subjects • p. 134

1 law

2 medicine

3 psychology

6 engineering

7 mathematics / math

4 business

5 education

8 information technology

9 nursing

10 architecture

NOW YOU CAN Get to know someone's life story

►5:24 CONVERSATION MODEL Read and listen.

A: Where were you born?
B: Here. In Houston.
A: And did you grow up here?
B: Yes, I did. And you?
A: I was born in Lima.
B: Did you grow up there?
A: Actually, no. I grew up in New York.

►5:25 RHYTHM AND INTONATION Listen again and repeat. Then practice the Conversation Model with a partner.

CONVERSATION ACTIVATOR With a partner, personalize the conversation with real information.

A: Where were you born?
B: ....
A: And did you grow up .... ?
B: .... And you?
A: I was born in ....
B: Did you grow up .... ?
A: ....

DON'T STOP!
Ask and answer more questions.

RECYCLE THIS LANGUAGE.
What do you do?
What are you studying?
   [or What did you study?]
Did you graduate?
How often did you move?

CHANGE PARTNERS Get to know another classmate's life story.

DIGITAL FLASH CARDS 1 ▶5:26 **VOCABULARY** • *More leisure activities* Read and listen. Then listen again and repeat.

VOCABULARY BOOSTER
More leisure activities • p. 134

1 travel

2 go camping

3 go fishing

4 relax

Also remember:
check e-mail
exercise
go dancing
go out for dinner
go running
go to the beach
go to the movies
listen to music
paint
play soccer
read
take a nap
visit friends

5 hang out with friends

6 sleep late

7 do nothing

2 ▶5:27 **LISTENING COMPREHENSION** Listen to the phone calls. Complete each sentence with the present continuous form of one of the words or phrases from the Vocabulary.

1 Charlie is *doing nothing* ....

2 Rachel's ....

3 They're .... on Saturday.

4 Barbara's ....

5 Harvey's family is ....

3 **GRAMMAR** • *Be going to + base form*

Use **be going to** + base form to express future plans.	**Contractions**
	is not going / **'s not going** / **isn't going**
	are not going / **'re not going** / **aren't going**

I'm
You're
He's
She's | going to relax this weekend.
We're
They're

I'm
You're
He's
She's | not going to go camping this weekend.
We're
They're

Yes / no questions

Are you **going to** sleep late tomorrow? Yes, I am. / No, I'm not.
Is she **going to** travel to Europe? Yes, she is. / No, she isn't.
Are we **going to** be on time? Yes, we are. / No, we aren't.

4 GRAMMAR PRACTICE Write sentences about future plans with <u>be going to</u>.

1 you / eat in a restaurant / this weekend? *Are you going to eat in a restaurant this weekend?*

2 They / go to the movies / tonight. ....

3 I / hang out with my parents / at the beach. ....

4 he / relax / tomorrow? ....

5 she / go fishing / with you? ....

6 we / exercise / on Saturday? ....

7 they / move? ....

8 Jeff and Joan / study / architecture. ....

9 She / graduate / in May. ....

NOW YOU CAN Discuss plans

▶5:28 **CONVERSATION MODEL** Read and listen.

A: Any plans for the weekend?
B: Not really. I'm just going to hang out with friends. And you?
A: Actually, I'm going to go camping.

▶5:29 **RHYTHM AND INTONATION** Listen again and repeat. Then practice the Conversation Model with a partner.

CONVERSATION ACTIVATOR With a partner, personalize the conversation. Use the Vocabulary or the pictures below and <u>be going to</u>.

A: Any plans for .... ?
B: .... I'm .... And you?
A: Actually, I'm ....

DON'T STOP!
Ask about other times. Ask more questions with <u>be going to</u>.

RECYCLE THIS LANGUAGE.
Are you going to ___ [tonight / tomorrow / next week / after class]?
How about [next weekend / the day after tomorrow]?

CHANGE PARTNERS Ask another classmate about his or her plans.

GOAL **Share your dreams for the future**

1 ▶5:30 VOCABULARY • *Some dreams for the future*   Read and listen. Then listen again and repeat.

1 I'd like to **get married**.   **2** I'd like to **have children**.   **3** I'd like to **retire**.   **4** I'd like to **change care**

5 I'd like to **travel**.   **6** I'd like to **make a lot of money**.   **7** I'd like to **give money to charity**.   **8** I'd like to **live a long life**.

2 ▶5:31 LISTENING COMPREHENSION   Listen and complete each sentence with the Vocabulary.

1 She'd like to ..*get married*.............. .   **5** She'd like to ....

2 He'd like to ....   **6** She'd like to ....

3 She'd like to ....   **7** He'd like to ....

4 He'd like to ....   **8** She'd like to ....

3 ACTIVATE VOCABULARY   Complete the survey by checking the boxes for your dreams for the future.

In the next two years, I'd like to...

- ☐ get married
- ☐ graduate
- ☐ travel
- ☐ have children
- ☐ move to a new country
- ☐ move to a new city
- ☐ move to a new apartment or a new house
- ☐ study a new language
- ☐ write a book
- ☐ make a lot of money
- ☐ give money to charity
- ☐ learn to play a musical instrument
- ☐ get a new car
- ☐ meet a good-looking man
- ☐ meet a good-looking woman
- ☐ change careers
- ☐ retire
- ☐ paint my living room
- ☐ buy a new refrigerator
- ☐ OTHER *I'd like to...*
  _____
  _____
  _____

4 VOCABULARY PRACTICE On the notepad, write three of your dreams from the survey on page 116.

> I'd like to move to a new city.

5 PAIR WORK Compare surveys with a partner. Ask and answer questions.

" I'd like to write a book. What about you? "

" Me? I'd like to change careers! "

NOW YOU CAN Share your dreams for the future

▶5:32 **CONVERSATION MODEL** Read and listen.

A: So what are your dreams for the future?
B: Well, I'd like to get married and have children. What about you?
A: Me? Actually, I'd like to study art.
B: Really? That's great.

▶5:33 **RHYTHM AND INTONATION** Listen again and repeat. Then practice the Conversation Model with a partner.

CONVERSATION ACTIVATOR With a partner, personalize the conversation. Use the Vocabulary from page 116 and real information.

A: So what are your dreams for the future?
B: Well, I'd like to .... What about you?
A: Me? Actually, I'd like to ....
B: Really? That's great.

DON'T STOP!
Talk about other plans.

 RECYCLE THIS LANGUAGE.

Really?
No kidding!
Sounds nice. / Sounds good.

CHANGE PARTNERS Ask another classmate what he or she would like to do.

1 ▶ 5:34 **READING** Read about Harry Houdini, a famous escape artist.

The Amazing
HOUDINI

Harry Houdini was born Ehrich Weisz in Budapest, Hungary, on March 24, 1874. He came from a large family. He had six siblings—five brothers and one sister.

At the age of four, Ehrich moved with his family to the United States, first to Appleton, Wisconsin, and then later to New York City.

The family was poor, and young Ehrich didn't get an education and never graduated from school. Instead, he worked to help the family. Ehrich and his brother Theo were interested in magic, and at the age of seventeen, Ehrich began his career as a magician. He changed his name to Houdini, after the name of a famous French magician, Robert Houdin.

In 1893, Houdini married Beatrice Raymond, whom he called Bess. For the rest of Houdini's career, Bess worked as his assistant on stage. The couple didn't have children.

At first, Houdini wasn't very successful. But in 1899, he started to do "escape acts," in which he escaped from chains and handcuffs. People came to see him escape from chains and boxes underwater. In one famous act, Houdini escaped from a large milk can filled with milk. Houdini became rich and famous all over the world.

In 1926, Houdini was sick during a performance. After the show, he went to the hospital. But it was too late—Harry Houdini died at the young age of 52.

HOUDINI PRESENTS HIS OWN ORIGINAL INVENTION THE GREATEST SENSATIONAL MYSTERY EVER ATTEMPTED IN THIS OR ANY OTHER AGE

$200 REWARD TO ANY ONE PROVING THAT IT IS POSSIBLE TO OBTAIN AIR IN THE UP-SIDE-DOWN POSITION IN WHICH HOUDINI RELEASES HIMSELF FROM THIS WATER-FILLED-TORTURE-CELL.

2 **READING COMPREHENSION** Answer the questions in complete sentences.

1 What was Houdini's original name? ....

2 Where was he born? ....

3 When did his family move? ....

4 Where did they move? ....

5 Did Houdini graduate from a university? ....

6 Did Houdini get married? ....

7 What was his wife's name? ....

8 Did the Houdinis have children? ....

9 When did Houdini die? ....

10 **Challenge:** Do you want to know more about Houdini? Write three information questions about Houdini. Example:

> Why did Houdini's family move to the United States?

GRAMMAR BOOSTER
Unit 14 review • p. 145

DIGITAL
MORE
EXERCISES

For additional language practice . . .

3 **PAIR WORK** Tell your partner your life story. Ask your partner questions about his or her story.

♫ **TOP NOTCH** **POP** • Lyrics p. 15
"I Wasn't Born Yesterday"

DIGITAL
SONG

DIGITAL
KARAOKE

Miranda Lewis
Born August 3, 1993
San Antonio (U.S.)

PAIR WORK Ask and answer questions about Miranda Lewis's life. Ask about her plans and her dreams for the future. For example:

Where was Miranda born?

TELL A STORY Tell the story of Miranda's life. Talk about the past, the present, and the future. What did she do? What is she doing now? What would she like to do? Start like this:

Miranda was born in 1993. She grew up in ...

WRITING Write the story of your own life and about your plans and dreams for the future. Include a picture or pictures if possible. For example:

I was born in Madrid in 1986. I grew up in ...

WRITING BOOSTER p. 149
Guidance for this writing exercise

1995–2008
Miranda's house
Atlanta (U.S.)

May 12, 2013
Millerton State Business College
Las Vegas (U.S.)

Next year she'd like...

In three years she'd like...

Miranda today
Los Angeles (U.S.)

NOW I CAN

☐ Get to know someone's life story.
☐ Discuss plans.
☐ Share my dreams for the future.

Units 8–14 REVIEW

1 ▶ 5:37 **LISTENING COMPREHENSION** Listen to the conversations. Check the picture that answers each question.

1 Where does he live?

a ☐   b ☐

2 Where does he work?

a ☐   b ☐

3 Where does she work?

a ☐   b ☐

4 Where does she teach?

a ☐   b ☐

5 Where does she work?

a ☐   b ☐

6 Where does his daughter work?

 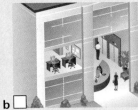

a ☐   b ☐

2 **VOCABULARY / GRAMMAR PRACTICE** Complete the e-mail about Anna's new apartment. Use <u>there's</u> and <u>there are</u> and the names of furniture and appliances.

● ● ●	My new apartment!

Hey, Mel: I have this great furnished apartment. It has everything!
The .... has a nice big stove and four ....
              1   2
There's a dining room with a .... and four ....
                                    3   4
Next to the dining room .... a large living room
                                    5
with a green .... And .... four chairs: great
                      6   7
for hanging out with my friends and watching ....
                                                          8
There's no office, but there's a .... in the
                                              9
living room. And I love the bedroom. It has a .... for
                                                    10
all my books. There are two .... and two blue
                                    11
.... Very nice! There's even a beautiful balcony
            12
next to the bedroom, with a little .... and two
                                              13
.... The bathroom is the only room that isn't perfect.
      14
.... a shower but no ....
      15   16

3 GRAMMAR PRACTICE Write questions about home and work. Use <u>What</u>, <u>Where</u>, <u>Is there</u>, and <u>Are there</u>. Answer the questions with true information.

Your questions	Your answers
1 Is there a closet in your bedroom?	1 Yes, there is.
2	2
3	3
4	4
5	5
6	6

4 GRAMMAR PRACTICE Complete the conversations with the correct forms of the verbs.

1 A: Where .... Jill .... last weekend?
　　　　　　　　　　　　go

B: I'm not sure. I know she .... to go
　　　　　　　　　　　　　　　　want
camping.

A: Maybe she .... camping, then.
　　　　　　　　　　go

2 A: Are you going to go to the beach today?

B: No way. We .... there yesterday.
　　　　　　　　　　be
We .... an awful time.
　　　　have

A: Why? What .... wrong?
　　　　　　　　　　be

B: The water .... really dirty, so I
　　　　　　　　　　be
.... swimming.
　not go

3 A: Where .... you this morning?
　　　　　　　　　be

B: Me? I .... running.
　　　　　　　go

A: Did Sheri .... with you?
　　　　　　　　　　go

B: No. She .... to class.
　　　　　　　go

4 A: .... you .... yesterday?
　　　　　　　　　　work

B: No, I .... Yesterday I .... sick.
　　　　　　　　　　　　　　　　be

A: I'm sorry. .... you .... a fever?
　　　　　　　　　　　　　　have

B: Yes, I ....

5 CONVERSATION PRACTICE Use the questions you wrote in Grammar Practice 3. Exchange real information about where you live and work. Start like this:

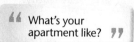

" What's your apartment like? "

Ideas
- the location of your home, school, and workplace
- the places in your neighborhood
- the description of your home

6 GRAMMAR PRACTICE Complete the telephone conversations with the present continuous or the simple present tense.

1 A: Hello?

  B: Hi, Sid. Ann. ....?
                                          you / sleep

  A: No, I'm not. .... breakfast.
                          I / make

  B: .... breakfast?
        you / usually / make

  A: Actually, ... often.
                   I / not cook

    But .... for a test.
             Gwen / study

2 A: Hello?

  B: Hi, Bonnie. .... for food.
                I / shop

    .... anything from the store?
      you / need

  A: Actually, yes. .... a salad for
                I / make

    dinner and .... any tomatoes.
             I / not have

  B: No problem. .... those
             They / sell

    beautiful tomatoes from Mexico right now.

  A: Great! .... those tomatoes.
            I / like

3 A: Hello?

  B: Hi, Liz. Where are you?

  A: .... right now. Can I
            I / drive

    call you back?

  B: Sure. .... my office
             you have

    number? .... today.
             I / work

4 A: Hello?

  B: Hi, Stan. What time ....
                     you / get up

    on Saturdays?

  A: Why .... that now
             you / ask

    It's only Thursday!

  B: Because .... her driving
             Maria / take

    test at 8:30, and .... a ride to
                she / need

    the test.

7 PAIR WORK Partner A: Look at your picture. Partner B: Turn your book and look at your picture. Ask questions about the foods on the table.

> 66 Are there any apples on your table? 99

> 66 No, there aren't. 99

PARTNER A

ARTNER B

8 GRAMMAR PRACTICE Write questions to complete each conversation.

1 A: ....?
  B: I usually eat lunch at the office.

2 A: ....?
  B: Dana and Eric? They went to Colorado.

3 A: ....?
  B: Milk? We need two large containers.

4 A: ....?
  B: Sally teaches math.

5 A: ....?
  B: Madhur was born in India.

6 A: ....
  B: No, I can't. I sing very badly.

7 A: ....
  B: No. I'm not going to graduate this year.

8 A: ....
  B: She broke her leg.

9 A: ....
  B: Oh, that's Scarlett Johansson, the actress.

10 A: ....
  B: Yes. My parents can speak Arabic, but I can

9 ▶5:38 **LISTENING COMPREHENSION** Listen to the conversations. Check Past, Present, or Future. Then listen again and check your work.

	Past	Present	Future
1	☐	☑	☐
2	☐	☐	☐
3	☐	☐	☐
4	☐	☐	☐
5	☐	☐	☐
6	☐	☐	☐

10 **VOCABULARY / GRAMMAR PRACTICE** Express sympathy to each person. Make suggestions with <u>should</u> and <u>shouldn't</u>.

1
I have a terrible headache.

YOU *I'm so sorry*............ You
should take something............
....

2
My husband is making lunch and he burned his hand!

YOU .... He
....
....

3
My brother and I have stomachaches. I think we ate something bad.

YOU .... You
....
....

4
My wife has a terrible backache!

YOU .... She
....
....

5
I didn't sleep last night. I feel terrible!

YOU .... You
....
....

6
My son has an earache and a fever. He's only eighteen months old.

YOU .... He
....
....

7
My grandfather fell down and broke his arm!

YOU .... He
....
....

11 **CONVERSATION PRACTICE** Discuss relatives and friends. Start like this:

Ideas
- Appearance
- Studies
- Abilities
- Life events
- Dreams for the future

❝ Tell me about your mother. Where was she born? ❞

🔁 **RECYCLE THIS LANGUAGE.**

And your [father]?
Really?
No kidding.

Reference Charts

COUNTRIES AND NATIONALITIES

Argentina	Argentinean / Argentine	Guatemala	Guatemalan	Peru	Peruvian
Australia	Australian	Holland	Dutch	Poland	Polish
Belgium	Belgian	Honduras	Honduran	Portugal	Portuguese
Bolivia	Bolivian	Hungary	Hungarian	Russia	Russian
Brazil	Brazilian	India	Indian	Saudi Arabia	Saudi / Saudi Arabian
Canada	Canadian	Indonesia	Indonesian	Spain	Spanish
Chile	Chilean	Ireland	Irish	Sweden	Swedish
China	Chinese	Italy	Italian	Switzerland	Swiss
Colombia	Colombian	Japan	Japanese	Taiwan	Chinese
Costa Rica	Costa Rican	Korea	Korean	Thailand	Thai
Ecuador	Ecuadorian	Lebanon	Lebanese	Turkey	Turkish
Egypt	Egyptian	Malaysia	Malaysian	the United Kingdom	British
El Salvador	Salvadorean	Mexico	Mexican	the United States	American
France	French	Nicaragua	Nicaraguan	Uruguay	Uruguayan
Germany	German	Panama	Panamanian	Venezuela	Venezuelan
Greece	Greek	Paraguay	Paraguayan	Vietnam	Vietnamese

NUMBERS 100 TO 1,000,000,000

100	one hundred	1,000	one thousand	10,000	ten thousand	1,000,000	one million
500	five hundred	5,000	five thousand	100,000	one hundred thousand	1,000,000,000	one billion

IRREGULAR VERBS

This is an alphabetical list of all irregular verbs in the *Top Notch Fundamentals* units.

base form	simple past	base form	simple past	base form	simple past
be	was / were	get	got	say	said
break	broke	give	gave	see	saw
bring	brought	go	went	sing	sang
buy	bought	grow	grew	sit	sat
choose	chose	hang out	hung out	sleep	slept
come	came	have	had	stand	stood
cut	cut	hear	heard	swim	swam
do	did	hurt	hurt	take	took
draw	drew	lie	lay	teach	taught
drink	drank	make	made	tell	told
drive	drove	meet	met	think	thought
eat	ate	put	put	throw	threw
fall	fell	read	read	wear	wore
feel	felt	ride	rode	write	wrote
find	found				

PRONUNCIATION TABLE

These are the pronunciation symbols used in *Top Notch Fundamentals*.

Vowels

Symbol	Key Words	Symbol	Key Words
i	feed	ə	banana, around
ɪ	did	ɚ	shirt, birthday
eɪ	date, table	aɪ	cry, eye
ɛ	bed, neck	aʊ	about, how
æ	bad, hand	ɔɪ	boy
ɑ	box, father	ɪr	here, near
ɔ	wash	ɛr	chair
oʊ	comb, post	ɑr	guitar, are
ʊ	book, good	ɔr	door, chore
u	boot, food, student	ʊr	tour
ʌ	but, mother		

Consonants

Symbol	Key Words	Symbol	Key Words
p	park, happy	t	butter, bottle
b	back, cabbage	tˀ	button
t	tie	ʃ	she, station, special, discussion
d	die		
k	came, kitchen, quarter	ʒ	leisure
g	game, go	h	hot, who
tʃ	chicken, watch	m	men
dʒ	jacket, orange	n	sun, know
f	face, photographer	ŋ	sung, singer
v	vacation	w	week, white
θ	thing, math	l	light, long
ð	then, that	r	rain, writer
s	city, psychology	y	yes, use, music
z	please, goes		

Vocabulary Booster

▶5:39 **MORE OCCUPATIONS**

1 an accountant

2 a bank teller

3 an electrician

4 a florist

5 a gardener

6 a grocery clerk

7 a hairdresser

8 a mechanic

9 a pharmacist

10 a professor

11 a reporter

12 a salesperson

13 a travel agent

14 a secretary

15 a server / a waiter

16 a nurse

17 a lawyer

> **Write five statements about the pictures.**
> **Use He or She and the verb be.**
> For example:
> *She's an accountant.*

▶ 5:40 **MORE RELATIONSHIPS**   ┆   ▶ 5:41 **MORE TITLES**

1 a supervisor *gonetici*
2 an employee *calßon*

3 teammates
Fakim orkodası

1 Doctor [Smith] or Dr. [Smith]

2 Professor [Brown]

3 Captain [Jones]

> Write two more statements about the photos in More Relationships, using <u>He's</u> or <u>She's</u> and possessive adjectives.
> For example: *He's her supervisor.*

UNIT 3

▶ 5:42 **MORE PLACES IN THE NEIGHBORHOOD**

1 a clothes store

2 an electronics store

3 a fire station

4 a police station

5 a shoe store

6 a toy store

7 a dry cleaners

8 a gas station

10 a supermarket

11 a convenience store

12 a travel agency

9 a hotel

13 a post office

14 a taxi stand

> Write five questions about the places
> For example:
> Where's the clothes store?
> Can I walk to the hotel?

▶ 5:43 **MORE ADJECTIVES TO DESCRIBE PEOPLE**

4 muscular

slim / thin

2 heavy

3 skinny

Write a sentence for each photo. Use a form of <u>be</u> and the adverb <u>very</u> or <u>so</u>.
For example:
She's very _____.

UNIT 5

5:44 **MORE EVENTS**

a ballet

2 an opera

3 an exhibition

4 a football game

6 a baseball game

7 a play

8 a speech / a talk

a volleyball game

On a separate sheet of paper, write five statements about the events. Use your own times, days, and dates.
For example:
There's a ballet on Tuesday, June 15 at 6:00 P.M.

UNIT 6

▶ 5:45 MORE CLOTHES

5   a hat

1   swimsuits /
    bathing suits

2   a bathrobe

3   a coat
4   boots

6   jeans

7   a nightgow

10   sandals

15   socks

16   underwear

8   an umbrella
9   a raincoat

14   pantyhose

11   pajamas

12   a T-shirt
13   shorts

> **Write five questions and answers about the colors of the clothes and shoes.**
>
> For example:
>
> *What color are the boots?*
> *They're brown.*

UNIT 7

▶ 5:46 MORE HOUSEHOLD CHORES

1   dust

2   sweep

3   mop

4   vacuum

> **Who does these chores in your house? Write four statements, using the simple present tense and frequency adverbs or time expressions.**
>
> For example: *I usually dust once a week.*

4 an intercom

5 a doorbell

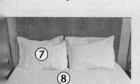

6 a fire escape

1 a roof
2 a fence
3 a driveway

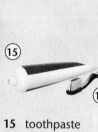

12 a faucet

15 toothpaste
16 a toothbrush

7 a pillow
8 a sheet
9 a blanket

10 a shower curtain
11 a bath mat

13 towels

14 a medicine cabinet

20 a coffee maker

21 a ladle
22 a pot

23 a food processor

7 a burner
8 an oven

19 a dishwasher

24 a napkin
25 a place mat
26 a glass

27 a fork
28 a knife
29 a tablespoon /
   a soup spoon
30 a teaspoon

31 a plate
32 a bowl

33 a cup
34 a saucer

a filing cabinet

36 a fax machine

Write five statements. Use the Vocabulary.

For example:

My apartment has a fire escape.
I have blue plates and bowls in my cabinets.

▶ 5:48 **MORE WEATHER VOCABULARY**

1 a thunderstorm

2 a snowstorm

3 a hurricane

4 a tornado

▶ 5:49 **THE FOUR SEASONS**

1 spring

2 summer

3 fall / autumn

4 winter

Write four statements about the weather and seasons pictures.

For example: It's not raining.

▶ 5:50 **MORE VEGETABLES**

1 carrots
2 brussels sprouts
3 leeks
4 cabbage
5 broccoli
6 cauliflower
7 lettuce
8 corn
9 peas
10 asparagus
11 cucumbers
12 an eggplant
13 beans
14 celery
15 garlic

▶ 5:51 **MORE FRUITS**

1 a grapefruit
2 a lime
3 a pineapple
4 grapes
5 a pear
6 an apricot
7 a peach
8 a strawberry
9 a raspberry
10 an avocado
11 a papaya
12 a mango
13 a kiwi
14 a watermelon
15 raisins
16 figs
17 prunes
18 dates

Write five statements about the fruits and vegetables you and your family like.

For example: *I like avocadoes. My sister doesn't like avocadoes.*

▶5:52 **MORE OUTDOOR ACTIVITIES**

1 go horseback riding

2 go sailing

3 play golf

4 go rollerblading

5 go snorkeling

> Write five sentences to describe the photos. Use the simple past tense.
> For example: *She went horseback riding.*

6 go rock climbing

7 go ice skating

8 go windsurfing

UNIT 12

▶5:53 **MORE PARTS OF THE BODY**

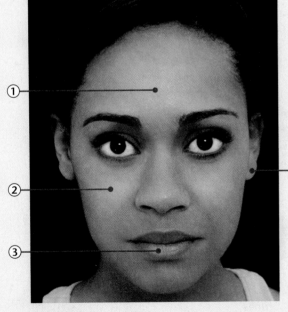

5 tongue

6 elbow
7 thigh
8 calf

1 forehead
2 cheek
3 lip
4 earlobe

> Describe one of the people. Write three statements. Use the Vocabulary from Unit 12
> For example: *She has straight brown hair.*

► 5:54 **MORE MUSICAL INSTRUMENTS**

a cello

2 a piano

3 a tuba

4 a trumpet

5 a trombone

6 a flute

7 a clarinet

9 a xylophone

10 a recorder

a saxophone

11 an accordion

12 drums

**Write four statements with the Vocabulary. Use
<u>can</u> / <u>can't</u> and the adverbs <u>well</u> and <u>badly</u>.**

For example:

My sister can play the piano well.
My father plays the accordion badly.

▶5:55 **MORE ACADEMIC SUBJECTS**

1 art

2 drama

3 science

4 biology

5 chemistry

Time line of 1480-1700-
Early modern period

6 history

▶5:56 **MORE LEISURE ACTIVITIES**

1 go skiing

2 go hiking

3 play

4 garden

5 go on a cruise

6 get a manicure

> Write four statements, using I'd like to or be going to and the Unit 14 Vocabulary. Include time expressions.
>
> For example:
>> I'd like to study fine art in the future.
>> I'm not going to go on a cruise this year

Grammar Booster

The Grammar Booster is optional. It contains extra practice of each unit's grammar.

UNIT 1

handwritten: 4 - 6 Sayfa

1 Write each sentence again. Use a contraction.

1 He is an engineer. _He's an engineer._
2 We are teachers. _We're teachrs._
3 No, we are not. _W. oren't_
4 They are not artists. _They're are not artsts_
5 I am a student. _I'm a student_
6 She is a chef. _She's a chef_

Write the indefinite article <u>a</u> or <u>an</u> for each occupation.

1 _a_ chef   5 _a_ scientist
2 _an_ actor   6 _an_ architect
3 _a_ banker   7 _a_ photographer
4 _a_ musician

Complete each sentence with the correct subject pronoun.

1 Mary is a student. _She_ is a student.
2 Ben is a student, too. _He_ is a student, too.
3 My name is Nora. _I_ am an artist.
4 Your occupation is doctor. _you_ are a doctor.
5 Jane and Jason are scientists. _They_ are scientists.

Write a question for each answer.

1 A: _Are you musicians?_ ?
   B: Yes, we are. We're musicians.
2 A: _Are they teachers_ ?
   B: No, they're not teachers. They're scientists.
3 A: _Is Ann a doctor_ ?
   B: Yes. Ann is a doctor.
4 A: _Is Ellen a writer_ ?
   B: No. Ellen is an architect. She's not a writer.
5 A: _You are a pilots_ ?
   B: Yes, I'm a pilot.
6 A: _____ ?
   B: No. We're not flight attendants. We're pilots.

Write six proper nouns and six common nouns. Use capital and lowercase letters correctly.

Proper nouns	Common nouns
1 New York City	7 a city
2	8
3	9
4	10
5	11
6	12

1 Write the correct possessive adjectives.

   1 Miss Kim is Mr. Smith's student. Mr. Smith is ..*her*......... teacher.

   2 Mr. Smith is Miss Kim's teacher. Miss Kim is .... student.

   3 Mrs. Krauss is John's teacher. Mrs. Krauss is .... teacher.

   4 John is Mrs. Krauss's student. John is .... student.

   5 Are .... colleagues from Japan? No, they aren't. My colleagues are from South Korea.

   6 Mr. Bello is .... teacher. I am .... student.

   7 Jake is not Mrs. Roy's student. He's .... boss!

   8 Mr. Gee is not Jim and Sue's teacher. He's .... doctor.

2 Complete the sentences about the people. Use <u>He's from</u>, <u>She's from</u>, or <u>They're from</u>.

   1 Ms. Tomiko Matsuda: ..*She's from*........ Hamamatsu, Japan.

   2 Miss Berta Soliz: .... Monterrey, Mexico.

   3 Mr. and Mrs. Franz Heidelberg: .... Berlin, Germany.

   4 Mr. George Crandall: .... Victoria, Canada.

   5 Ms. Mary Mellon: .... Melbourne, Australia.

   6 Mr. Jake Hild and Ms. Betty Parker: .... Los Angeles, U.S.

   7 Mr. Cui Jing Wen: .... Wuhan, China.

   8 Ms. Noor Bahjat: .... Cairo, Egypt.

3 Complete the questions. Begin each question with a capital letter.

   1 ..*What's*..... your name?

   2 .... are you from?

   3 .... his e-mail address?

   4 .... she a student?

   5 .... her phone number?

   6 .... they colleagues?

   7 .... he from China?

   8 .... their first names?

4 Complete each question with the correct possessive adjective.

   1 **A:** What's ..*your*........ name?

      B: I'm Mrs. Barker.

   2 **A:** What's .... last name?

      B: My last name is Lane.

   3 **A:** What's .... address?

      B: Mr. Marsh's address is 10 Main Street.

   4 **A:** What's .... e-mail address?

      B: Ms. Down's e-mail address? It's down5@unet.com.

   5 **A:** What are .... first names?

      B: They're Gary and Rita.

   6 **A:** What's .... phone number?

      B: Miss Gu's number is 555-0237.

UNIT 3

1 Write the sentences with contractions.

1 Where is the pharmacy? *Where's the pharmacy?* ....

2 It is down the street. ....

3 It is not on the right. ....

4 What is your name? ....

5 What is your e-mail address? ....

6 She is an architect. ....

7 I am a teacher. ....

8 You are my friend. ....

9 He is her neighbor. ....

10 They are my classmates. ....

2 Complete each sentence with an affirmative or a negative imperative. Begin each sentence with a capital letter.

1 Take the bus to the restaurant. *Don't walk.*

2 Don't walk. .... the bus to the bank.

3 .... to the restaurant. It's right over there, on the right.

4 .... a taxi to the bank. It's across the street.

3 Complete the questions and answers. Use subject pronouns and use contractions when possible.

1 A: *Where's* .... the pharmacy?

B: The pharmacy? .... across the street.

2 A: .... the newsstand?

B: .... down the street on the right.

3 A: .... I .... to the restaurant?

B: No, don't walk. .... a taxi.

4 A: .... do you go to school?

B: Me? I go .... motorcycle.

UNIT 4

1 Write questions. Use Who's or Who are and he, she, or they.

1 A: *Who's he* ....?

B: He's my grandfather.

2 A: ....?

B: She's my mother.

3 A: ....?

B: He's Mr. Ginn's grandson.

4 A: ....?

B: They're Ms. Breslin's grandparents.

5 A: ....?

B: She's Sam's wife.

6 A: ....?

B: They're his wife and son.

2　Unscramble the words and write sentences. Use <u>is</u> or <u>are</u>. Begin each sentence with a capital letter.

1　so / father / my / handsome ...*My father is so handsome.*...................................
2　brother / very / her / short ....
3　grandchildren / cute / neighbor's / so / my ....
4　his / tall / not / sister / very ....
5　grandfather / very / old / my / not ....
6　girlfriend / pretty / so / brother's / my ....

3　Complete the sentences. Use <u>have</u> or <u>has</u>.

1　I ...*have*........ two brothers.
2　She .... one child.
3　They .... four grandchildren.
4　We .... six children.
5　You .... ten brothers and sisters!
6　He .... three sisters.

4　Complete the questions. Use <u>How old is</u> or <u>How old are</u>.

1　...*How old are*........... your children?
2　................................. his son?
3　................................. her grandchildren?
4　................................. Nancy's sisters?
5　................................. Matt's daughter?
6　................................. their grandmother?

UNIT 5

1　Write a question for each answer. Use <u>What time</u>, <u>What day</u>, or <u>When</u>. Use a question mark (?).

1　...*What time is it?*...... It's 6:30.
2　................................. The party is at ten o'clock.
3　................................. The dinner is on Friday.
4　................................. The dance is at 11:30 on Saturday.
5　................................. The concert is in May.
6　................................. The meeting is at noon.
7　................................. It's a quarter to two.
8　................................. The movie is on Wednesday.

2　Complete each sentence with <u>in</u>, <u>on</u>, or <u>at</u>.

1　The concert is ...*in*.......... March.
2　The dinner is .... Friday .... 6:00.
3　The party is .... April 4ᵗʰ .... 9:00.
4　The movie is .... 3:00 P.M. .... Tuesday.
5　The game is .... noon .... Monday.
6　The meeting is .... August 10ᵗʰ .... 9:00 A.M.

UNIT 6

1 Complete each sentence with the correct form of the verb.

1 They ..._have_............... nice ties at this store.

       have

2 She .... a long blue skirt for the party.

       want

3 I .... my shoes.

    like

4 We .... clean shirts.

    not have

5 Our children .... blue pants for school.

    not need

6 .... short skirts?

    she / like

7 .... new shoes?

    your wife / need

8 .... a suit for work?

    I / need

9 Why .... those old shoes?

    she / like

10 Which shirt .... for tomorrow?

    you / want

11 .... this sweater in extra large?

    they / have

Choose <u>this</u>, <u>that</u>, <u>these</u>, or <u>those</u>.

1 I like (this / these) red sweaters.
2 I don't like (this / these) skirt. It's too long.
3 Why do you want (that / those) black pants?
4 (That / These) skirt is great for the school concert.

Answer each question with true answers. Begin each answer with a capital letter. End with a period (.)

1 What clothes do you need? ....
2 Do you need new shoes? ....
3 Do you have a long skirt? ....
4 Do you like pink shirts? ....
5 Do you have a loose sweater? ....
6 Do you like expensive clothes? ....

UNIT 7

Write the third-person singular form of each verb.

1 shave _shaves_..............
2 brush ....
3 go ....
4 have ....
5 study ....
6 do ....
7 take ....
8 play ....
9 exercise ....
10 visit ....
11 practice ....
12 wash ....

13 come ....
14 change ....
15 make ....
16 get ....
17 comb ....
18 put ....
19 eat ....
20 watch ....
21 clean ....
22 read ....
23 check ....
24 listen ....

2 Complete each question with <u>do</u> or <u>does</u>.

1 When ...<u>do</u>........... you go shopping?
2 What time .... she make dinner?
3 How often .... they clean the house?
4 What time .... your son come home?
5 How often .... your parents go out for dinner?
6 What time .... you go to bed?
7 When .... our teacher check e-mail?
8 How often .... Alex do the laundry?

3 Unscramble the words and write sentences in the simple present tense. Begin each sentence with a capital letter. End with a period (.).

1 usually / on weekends / go shopping / she ..*She usually goes shopping on weekends.*........
2 go dancing / my sisters / on Fridays / sometimes ....
3 in the morning / never / check e-mail / I ....
4 always / my daughter/ to work / take the bus ....
5 we / to school / walk / never ....
6 sometimes / my brother / after work / visit his friends ....

4 Complete each response with <u>do</u> or <u>does</u>.

1 Who takes out the garbage in your house? My daughter ..<u>does</u>.........
2 Who washes the dishes in your family? I ....
3 Who makes dinner? My parents ....
4 Who does the laundry in your house? My brother ....
5 Who watches TV before dinner? My granddaughter ....
6 Who takes a bath in the evening? My sister ....

UNIT 8

1 Write questions with <u>Where</u>. Use a question mark (?).

1 your grandparents / live ..*Where do your grandparents live?*........
2 John's friend / go shopping ....
3 her brother / study English ....
4 you / eat breakfast ....
5 they / listen to music ....
6 Rob and Nancy / exercise ....
7 his mother / work ....
8 your brother / do the laundry ....

2 Complete the statements with <u>in</u>, <u>on</u>, <u>at</u>, or <u>to</u>.

1 His house is ..<u>on</u>........... Barker Street.
2 They work .... the tenth floor.
3 Ms. Cruz takes the train .... work.
4 It's .... 18 Spencer Street.
5 Jack studies French .... the BTI Institute.
6 Mr. Klein works .... the hospital.
7 Ms. Anderson's office is .... the fifth floor.
8 Jason's sister works .... 5 Main Street.

3 Complete each sentence with <u>There's</u> or <u>There are</u>.

1 ...*There's*..... a movie at noon.
2 .... a concert at 2:00 and a game at 3:00.
3 .... a bank on the corner of Main and 12th Street.
4 .... two apartment buildings across the street.
5 .... bookstores nearby.
6 .... a pharmacy and a newsstand around the corner.
7 .... two dressers in the bedroom.
8 .... three elevators in the Smith Building.

4 Write questions with <u>Is there</u> or <u>Are there</u>. Use a question mark (?).

1 a dance / this weekend ..*Is there a dance this weekend?*...
2 three meetings / this week ....
3 a bank / nearby ....
4 how many / games / this afternoon ....
5 how many / pharmacies / on 3rd Avenue ....
6 how many / parties / this month ....

UNIT 9

Write the present participle of the following base forms.

1 rain ..*raining*.................
2 snow ....
3 watch ....
4 eat ....
5 take ....
6 drive ....
7 check ....
8 make ....
9 do ....
10 exercise ....
11 shave ....
12 put ....
13 comb ....
14 brush ....

15 come ....
16 wear ....
17 shop ....
18 go ....
19 study ....
20 listen ....
21 wash ....
22 play ....
23 read ....
24 clean ....
25 work ....
26 write ....
27 talk ....
28 buy ....

Check (✓) the sentences that indicate a future plan.

☑ 1 On Tuesday I'm working at home.
☐ 2 I'm watching TV right now.
☐ 3 Is Marina taking a shower?
☐ 4 Where is she going tomorrow night?
☐ 5 Jen's eating dinner.
☐ 6 I'm driving to the mall this afternoon.
☐ 7 I'm studying Arabic this year. My teacher is very good.
☐ 8 Who's making dinner on Saturday?

3 Complete each conversation with the present continuous.

1 A: *What are you doing* ....?
$\qquad$ what / you / do

B: .... my hair.
$\qquad$ I / wash

2 A: .... ?
$\qquad$ where / she / drive

B: .... to the bookstore.
$\qquad$ she / go

3 A: .... the bus?
$\qquad$ why / he / take

B: Because ....
$\qquad$ it / rain

4 A: .... at home tonight?
$\qquad$ we / eat

B: No. .... out for dinner.
$\qquad$ we / go

5 A: .... a dress to the party?
$\qquad$ Maya / wear

B: No. .... a dress. .... pants.
$\qquad$ she / not wear   she / wear

UNIT 10

1 Complete each question with <u>How much</u> or <u>How many</u>.

1 *How much* .... sugar do you want in your coffee?
2 .... onions do you need for the potato pancakes?
3 .... cans of coffee are there on the shelf?
4 .... meat do you eat every day?
5 .... loaves of bread do we need for dinner?
6 .... pepper would you like in your chicken salad?
7 .... bottles of oil does she need from the store?
8 .... eggs do you eat every week?
9 .... oranges are there? I want to make orange juice.
10 .... pasta would you like?

2 Choose the correct word or phrase to complete each statement. Circle the letter.

1 I .... English every day.
  a am studying   **b** study

2 We usually .... the bus to work.
  a are taking   **b** take

3 Annemarie .... the kitchen now.
  a is cleaning   **b** cleans

4 He really .... lemonade.
  a is liking   **b** likes

5 This store .... beautiful clothes.
  a is having   **b** has

6 On Wednesdays I .... dinner for my parents.
  a am cooking   **b** cook

7 They never .... coffee.
  a are drinking   **b** drink

8 Our children .... TV on weekdays.
  a are watching   **b** don't watch

UNIT 11

1 Complete the conversations with the past tense of <u>be</u>.

1 A: Where ..<u>were</u>........ Paul and Jackie last night?

B: I don't know, but they .... here.

2 A: .... she at school yesterday?

B: No. She .... at home.

3 A: When .... you in Italy? Last year?

B: Last year? No, we .... in Italy last year.
We .... there in 2012.

4 A: What time .... the movie?

B: It .... at 7:00.

5 A: .... your parents at home at 10:00 last night?

B: No. They .... at a play.

6 A: Who .... at work on Monday?

B: Barry and Anne .... But I ....

2 First complete each question. Use the simple past tense. Then write a true answer.
Begin each answer with a capital letter. End with a period (.).

1 ..<u>Did</u>........ you ..<u>go</u>.......... to work yesterday?
go

YOU ....

2 What time .... you .... dinner?
make

YOU ....

3 What .... you .... for breakfast?
eat

YOU ....

4 Who .... breakfast with you?
eat

YOU ....

5 What .... you .... this week?
buy

YOU ....

UNIT 12

Write (a) a sentence with <u>be</u> and (b) a sentence with <u>have</u>. Use a period (.)

1 Kate / hair / long / straight   **a** <u>Kate's hair is long and straight.</u>...........................

                                  b <u>Kate has long straight hair.</u>...........................

2 George / short / black / hair   **a** ....

                                  b ....

3 Harry / long / curly / hair   **a** ....

                                  b ....

4 Mary / eyes / blue   **a** ....

                                  b ....

5 Adam / beard / gray   **a** ....

                                  b ....

6 Amy / pretty / eyes   **a** ....

                                  b ....

2 Complete each sentence with <u>should</u> and a verb from the box.

1 It's your birthday. You ...*should go*........... out for dinner!

2 I'm sorry you have a toothache. You .... a dentist.

3 There's a movie on TV tonight. We .... it.

4 You have a cold? You .... today.

5 We have tomatoes, potatoes, and onions. We ....
tomato potato soup for dinner tonight!

6 Pam's taking a shower right now. You .... back later.

7 Martin has a headache. He .... soccer tonight.

8 It's time for bed. You .... undressed.

| call |
| (not) exercise |
| go |
| watch |
| make |
| (not) play |
| see |
| get |

UNIT 13

1 Write sentences with the simple present tense and the adverbs <u>well</u> or <u>badly</u>. Begin each sentence
with a capital letter. End with a period (.).

1 my father / sing / really well ..*My father sings really well.*................................

2 my mother / cook French food / well ....

3 my grandfather / play the guitar / badly ....

4 my grandmother / sew clothes / very well ....

5 my sister / knit sweaters / well ....

6 my friend / draw pictures / really well ....

7 I / play the violin / badly ....

2 Answer each question with true information. Use short answers with <u>can</u> or <u>can't</u>. Begin each
answer with a capital letter. End with a period (.)

1 Can you play the piano? ....

2 Can you ski? ....

3 Can your parents sing well? ....

4 Can your friends speak English? ....

5 Can you draw? ....

6 Can your father fix things? ....

3 Complete each sentence. Use <u>too</u> and an adjective.

1 I need a new dress. This dress is ..*too old*................. .

2 This skirt is .... I want a short skirt.

3 His shirt is .... He needs size small.

4 I don't want that suit. It's ....

5 He needs size medium. This shirt is ....

Answer the following questions with true information. Use <u>be going to</u>. Begin each answer with
a capital letter. End with a period (.).

1 Are your classmates going to study tonight? ....

2 Are you going to relax this weekend? ....

3 Are you going to exercise today? ....

4 Are you going to make dinner tonight? ....

5 Are you going to move in the next two years? ....

6 Are you going to check your e-mail today? ....

7 Are you going to hang out with your friends or family this weekend? ....

Write a question with <u>be going to</u> for each answer. Don't use the verb <u>do</u>. Begin each question with
a capital letter. End with a question mark (?).

1 ..*Are you going to go to the movies tonight?*.............. Yes. I'm going to go to the movies tonight.

2 .... Yes. They're going to eat in a restaurant after the concert.

3 .... Yes. Carla's brother is going to go fishing with her.

4 .... Yes. I'm going to go to work tomorrow.

5 .... No. He's not going to graduate this year.

6 .... Yes. They're going to take the bus to school.

Writing Booster

The Writing Booster is optional. It gives guidance for the writing task on the last page of each unit.

UNIT 1

Guided Writing Practice Look at the picture on page 11. Answer the questions, based on the picture. Write five sentences.

Is Martin a flight attendant?
Is he a musician?
Is Tim a musician?
Is he a manager?
Is Marie a flight attendant?

Example: *No. He's not a flight attendant.*

1	
2	
3	
4	
5	

UNIT 2

Guided Writing Practice Write sentences about your relationships.

Example: Write about a friend: *Ryan is my friend. He's a student, too. His last name is Grant.*

1 Write about a friend:	
2 Write about a classmate:	
3 Write about a neighbor:	
4 Write about a boss, colleague, or teacher:	

UNIT 3

Guided Writing Practice Look at the picture on page 27. Write five questions and answers, based on the picture.

Example: **Q:** *Where's the bank?*   **Q:** *Is the bank next to the . . .*
         A: *It's next to the restaurant.*   **A:** *No, it isn't. It's . . .*

1 Q:	
A:	
2 Q:	
A:	
3 Q:	
A:	
4 Q:	
A:	
5 Q:	
A:	

UNIT 4

Guided Writing Practice Choose two relatives. Write about each person.
Answer some of these questions.

How old is [he / she]?

Is [he / she] tall or short?

Is [he / she] old or young?

Is [he / she] good-looking? cute?

What's [his / her] occupation?

Example: *My sister is 24 years old. She's short and good-looking. She's an architect.*

1	
2	

UNIT 5

Guided Writing Practice Look at the event announcements on pages 42 and 43.
Choose five events. Write sentences about the events below.

Example: The birthday party: *The birthday party is at Chuck's Café. Chuck's Café is around the corner from the bank.*

The movie
The meeting
The dance
The volleyball game
The basketball game
The dinner
The "Evening" concert
The "welcome" party

UNIT 6

Guided Writing Practice Answer some or all of the following questions. Put the sentences together
to write about clothes you need, you want, and you like, and about clothes you have or don't have.

Do you want new clothes? Why?   What clothes do you need?   What colors do you like?

Do you need new clothes? Why?   What size do you need?

Example:

I need new clothes! I need a sweater, and I need new shoes, too. I want a white sweater and black shoes. Why? My white sweater is old and my black shoes are dirty. I need the sweater in large and the shoes in size 40.

UNIT 7

Guided Writing Practice Answer the questions about your typical week. Use time expressions and frequency adverbs.

What do you do in the morning?

What do you do in the afternoon?

What do you do in the evening?

What do you do on Saturdays and Sundays?

Example: In the morning, I usually get up at 7:00. Then I . . .

UNIT 8

Guided Writing Practice Choose one of the homes in the Reading on page 70. Write the features of that home and your home in the chart.

On a separate sheet of paper, compare the two homes in the chart. Use <u>and</u> and <u>but</u>.

Example:

Eduardo's home is an apartment, and I live in an apartment, too. There's an elevator in his building, but we don't have an elevator. In his apartment, there are . . .

	his or her home	my home
Is it a house or apartment?		
How many bedrooms are there?		
How many bathrooms are there?		
Is the kitchen small or large?		
Is there an office?		
Is there a garage or an elevator?		
Is there a garden?		
Is there a view?		
Other features?		

UNIT 9

Guided Writing Practice Write answers to some or all of the following questions about your plans for the week. Use time expressions.

What are you doing right now?

What are you doing this evening?

What are you doing tomorrow?

Are you doing anything special this weekend?

What are you doing on Saturday and Sunday?

Example:

Right now, I'm writing about my plans for the week. This evening, I'm checking e-mail and . . .

UNIT 10

Guided Writing Practice Answer some or all of the questions to help you write what you eat on a typical day. Use frequency adverbs <u>sometimes</u>, <u>usually</u>, and <u>always</u>. Use time expressions <u>every day</u>, <u>once a week</u>, <u>twice a week</u>, etc.

What do you eat for breakfast on weekdays?

What do you eat for breakfast on weekends?

What time do you usually eat your meals?

Do you eat after school or work?

How many times a week (or month) do you go out for dinner?

Example: On weekdays, I usually eat breakfast at 9:00. I always eat bread and eggs, and . . .

UNIT 11

Guided Writing Practice Write about your weekend. Use past time expressions. Answer some or all of the questions to guide your writing.

Did you have a good time last weekend?

How was the weather?

What did you do on Friday night?

What did you do on Saturday?

What did you do on Sunday?

Example: Last weekend, I had a great time . . .

UNIT 12

Guided Writing Practice Choose a person you want to describe. On a separate sheet of paper, answer the questions in your description.

Who is this person?

How old is the person?

Is he or she tall or short?

Is he or she good-looking?

What color is his or her hair?

Is it short or long? Straight, wavy, or curly?

What color are his or her eyes?

Does he or she wear glasses?

Example:

Mary Blake is my classmate, and she is twenty years old. She's very tall and pretty, and . . .

UNIT 13

Guided Writing Practice What can people do when they are eighty years old? Complete the chart. Then use the information from the chart to write about the topic. Write on a separate sheet of paper. Write as much as you can.

Example: Old people can't do some things, but sometimes they can . . .

	Yes, they can.	They can sometimes.	No, they can't.
work	☐	☐	☐
cook meals	☐	☐	☐
live on the second floor	☐	☐	☐
get dressed	☐	☐	☐
take a shower or bath	☐	☐	☐
clean the house	☐	☐	☐
exercise / go running / go bike riding	☐	☐	☐
drive a car	☐	☐	☐
go dancing	☐	☐	☐
other	☐	☐	☐

UNIT 14

Guided Writing Practice Write the story of your own life. Then write your plans and dreams for the future. Answer some or all of the following questions in your story. Write on a separate sheet of paper. Write as much as you can.

Where were you born?

Where do you live now?

Where did you grow up?

What school did you go to?

What did you study? (Or what are you studying now?)

Did you graduate?

What are your dreams for the future? (Write *I'd like . . .*)

Example: I was born on September 3rd, 1999 in . . .

Top Notch Pop Lyrics

▶ 1:30/1:31 **What Do You Do?** [Unit 1]

(CHORUS)
What do you do?
What do you do?

I'm a student.
You're a teacher.
She's a doctor.
He's a nurse.
What about you?
What do you do?
I'm a florist.
You're a gardener.
He's a waiter.
She's a chef.
Do-do-do-do…
That's what we do.
It's nice to meet you.
What's your name?
Can you spell that, please?
Thank you.
Yes, it's nice to meet you, too.

(CHORUS)

We are artists and musicians,
architects, and electricians.
How about you?
What do you do?
We are bankers,
we are dentists,
engineers, and flight attendants.
Do-do-do-do…
That's what we do.
Hi, I'm Linda. Are you John?
No, he's right over there.
Excuse me. Thank you very much.
Good-bye.
Do-do-do-do…
Do-do-do-do…
Do-do-do-do…
Do-do-do-do…

▶ 1:46/1:47 **Excuse Me, Please** [Unit 2]

(CHORUS)
Excuse me—please excuse me.
What's your number?
What's your name?
I would love to get to know you,
and I hope you feel the same.

I'll give you my e-mail address.
Write to me at my dot-com.
You can send a note in English
so I'll know
who it came from.
Excuse me—please excuse me.
Was that 0078?
Well, I think the class is starting,
and I don't
want to be late.

But it's really nice to meet you.
I'll be seeing you again.
Just call me on my cell phone
when you're looking for a friend.

(CHORUS)

So welcome to the classroom.
There's a seat right over there.
I'm sorry, but you're sitting in
our teacher's favorite chair!
Excuse me—please excuse me.
What's your number?
What's your name?

▶ 2:15/2:16 **Tell Me All About It** [Unit 4]

Tell me about your father.
He's a doctor and he's very tall.
And how about your mother?
She's a lawyer. That's her picture on
the wall.
Tell me about your brother.
He's an actor, and he's twenty-three.
And how about your sister?
She's an artist. Don't you think she looks
like me?

(CHORUS)
Tell me about your family—
who they are and what they do.
Tell me all about it.
It's so nice to talk with you.

Tell me about your family.
I have a brother and a sister, too.
And what about your parents?
Dad's a teacher, and my mother's eyes
are blue.

(CHORUS)

Who's the pretty girl in that photograph?
That one's me!
You look so cute!
Oh, that picture makes me laugh!
And who are the people there, right below
that one?
Let me see … that's my mom and dad.
They both look very young.

(CHORUS)

Tell me all about it.
Tell me all about it.

▶ 2:35/2:36 **Let's Make a Date** [Unit 5]

It's early in the evening—
6:15 P.M.
Here in New York City
a summer night begins.
I take the bus at seven
down the street from City Hall.
I walk around the corner
when I get your call.

(CHORUS)
Let's make a date.
Let's celebrate.
Let's have a great time out.

Let's meet in the Village
on Second Avenue
next to the museum there.
What time is good for you?
It's a quarter after seven.
There's a very good new show
weekdays at the theater.
Would you like to go?

(CHORUS)

Sounds great. What time's the show?
The first one is at eight.
And when's the second one?
The second show's too late.
OK, how do I get there?
The trains don't run at night.
No problem. Take a taxi.
The place is on the right.
Uh-oh! Are we late?
No, we're right on time.
It's 7:58.
Don't worry. We'll be fine!

(CHORUS)

▶ 3:15/3:16 **On the Weekend** [Unit 7]

(CHORUS)
On the weekend,
when we go out,
there is always so much joy and laughter
On the weekend,
we never think about
the days that come before and after.

He gets up every morning.
Without warning, the bedside clock rings
the alarm.
So he gets dressed—
he does his best to be on time.
He combs his hair, goes down the stairs,
and makes some breakfast.
A bite to eat, and he feels fine.
Yes, he's on his way
to one more working day.

(CHORUS)

On Thursday night,
when he comes home from work,
he gets undressed, and if his room's a mess
he cleans the house. Sometimes he takes
a rest.
Maybe he cooks something delicious,
and when he's done
he washes all the pots and dishes,
then goes to bed.
He knows the weekend's just ahead.

(CHORUS)